THE ESSENTIAL HR GUIDE FOR SMALL BUSINESSES AND STARTUPS

THE ESSENTIAL HR GUIDE FOR SMALL BUSINESSES AND STARTUPS

Best Practices, Tools, Examples, and Online Resources

Marie Carasco

William J. Rothwell

Society for Human Resource Management
Alexandria, Virginia I shrm.org
Society for Human Resource Management, India Office
Mumbai, India I shrmindia.org
Society for Human Resource Management, Middle East and Africa Office
Dubai, UAE I shrm.org/pages/mena.aspx

This book is published by the Society for Human Resource Management (SHRM). The interpretations, conclusions, and recommendations in this book are those of the author and do not necessarily represent those of the publisher.

SHRM, the Society for Human Resource Management, creates better workplaces where employers and employees thrive together. As the voice of all things work, workers and the workplace, SHRM is the foremost expert, convener and thought leader on issues impacting today's evolving workplaces. With 300,000+ HR and business executive members in 165 countries, SHRM impacts the lives of more than 115 million workers and families globally. Learn more at SHRM.org and on Twitter @SHRM.

Library of Congress Cataloging-in-Publication Data

Names: Carasco, Marie, author. | Rothwell, William J., 1951- author.
Title: The essential HR guide for small businesses and startups : best
   practices, tools, examples, and online resources / Marie Carasco,
   William J. Rothwell.
Description: Alexandria : Society for Human Resource Management, 2020. |
   Includes bibliographical references and index.
Identifiers: LCCN 2019053057 | ISBN 9781586445898 (paperback)
Subjects: LCSH: Small business--Management. | New business
   enterprises--Management. | Personnel management.
Classification: LCC HD62.7 .C3547 2020 | DDC 658.3--dc23

Printed in the United States of America

PB Printing 10 9 8 7 6 5 4 3 2 1   61.19305

Marie Carasco *dedicates this book to her family, mentors, and friends, both old and new. Especially those who've loved and valued her presence.*

William J. Rothwell *dedicates this book to his wife, Marcelina V. Rothwell. She is the wind beneath his wings.*

Brief Contents

PART I
HR FUNDAMENTALS FOR STARTUP AND EARLY STAGE BUSINESSES

PART II
LEGAL AND WORKFORCE PLANNING FOR GROWTH STAGE BUSINESSES

Contents

PART I

HR FUNDAMENTALS FOR STARTUP AND EARLY STAGE BUSINESSES

PART II

LEGAL AND WORKFORCE PLANNING FOR GROWTH STAGE BUSINESSES

CHAPTER 4

Legal 73

List of Figures, Tables, and Exhibits

FIGURES

TABLES

EXHIBITS

Foreword

The reality for several entrepreneurs when they set out to start their business is they may not have the network, financial resources, and/or some of the professional skills necessary to launch, operate, and/or grow the business. They start their companies with a dream and a passion for what they believe is a good idea, service, or product. They learn how to manage and operate their business by way of trial by fire. That process may lead to costly mistakes. The hope is that at some point during their journey, someone or something has the answers to help. *The Essential HR Guide for Small Businesses and Startups* is the ideal book for startups and small businesses who have identified the importance of people to their company.

One of the keys to success in any organization, whether it be a startup, an existing small business, or a growth phased business, is having good people at every level. As a member of the advisory committee involved in shaping the content of this book, this resource has become increasingly important because it provides essential guidance and solutions to the often-unanswered questions posed by business owners related to human resource management. For the past 20 years, my professional life has been immersed in the world of entrepreneurship, from educating, consulting, and working for small business owners, to launching companies of my own. Over the years, the topic of human resource management has been a Pandora's box. Many new entrepreneurs and experienced business owners have not embraced or grasped the concepts in human resource management. For some, it's compliance. For others, it's the process of hiring people and managing payroll. However, these and other related human resource topics are areas of the business where an entrepreneur, small business owner, or manager will not find the answers they need from an Internet search.

First, talent or human capital is interwoven throughout the entire organization, and without understanding the big picture, any single approach can send ripple effects through the company. Second, no two companies are exactly the same, and the dynamics of acquiring, training, developing, retaining, and managing people are skills that not only need to be obtained and developed, but also tailored. Before an entrepreneur can expect employees to share and connect to the vision and mission of their business, they will need to understand how to do so. *The Essential HR Guide for Small Businesses and Startups* will help lay a foundational understanding of how to attract, compensate, manage, and train your current and future talent, as well as how to align employees with the overall goals of your company using practical tools you can implement immediately.

The Essential HR Guide for Small Businesses and Startups should be read by anyone in a position to recruit, hire, manage, and/or promote talent in a startup, early stage, or small business. This includes founders, business owners, middle management, senior managers, HR officers, or those with HR responsibilities. This book is especially valuable to those with limited experience with HR, have few resources, and are seeking to build and grow their organization responsibly using proven methods, tactics, and tools to structure and manage human capital in their business.

Marie Carasco and William J. Rothwell are the ideal authors for this book because they not only have expertise in human resource management, strategic workforce planning, and managing change, but they also both own and operate small businesses. This book is written through the lens of an entrepreneur. It concisely and effectively considers and addresses the unique challenges faced by owners. *The Essential HR Guide for Small Businesses and Startups* captures the dynamics experienced by managers and HR personnel working for a small business owner, and outlines the key procedures and processes needed to operate and support a startup, early stage, or small business. It will become evident when reading this book that the content bridges the gap between human resource theory and application. The reader doesn't need a formal business background, education, or training to leverage the tools and resources provided. After completing this book, the reader will be knowledgeable and empowered to develop, implement, and manage all things human resource related in a startup, early stage, or small business.

My hope is *The Essential HR Guide for Small Businesses and Startups* will become the go-to tool that every entrepreneur utilizes when starting or growing their business. The answers to questions like "How do I pay someone when I don't have any money?," "When should I hire someone full time?," and "How do I build culture?" will be found with additional resources in *The Essential HR Guide for Small Businesses and Startups.*

—Rod Dauphin, MBA
Education Services Director
Goldman Sachs 10,000 Small Businesses Initiative
LaGuardia Community College

Preface

Natalie Robehmed outlined key aspects of startups in her 2013 *Forbes* article entitled "What Is A Startup?" Startups are companies that generate less than $20 million, have fewer than 80 employees, have been in business for less than 10 years, and the founders of the company remain in control. A business is no longer considered a startup when these factors increase, the company has more than one office, the business becomes profitable, the company is sold or acquired by a larger company, the organization has over five people on the board, or the founders have sold personal shares.

Our interest is to highlight and help strategically address the unique people-related challenges faced by startups and small businesses. To do so, this book is grounded in the experiences of startup founders, small business educators, and human resources leaders who have worked with and through startup, early stage, and small business organizations.

Chapter 1—Talent: How to Attract, Find, and Train It provides strategies to find and onboard the best people to work in a startup environment based on the needs of the business, as well as ways to build a positive culture.

Chapter 2—Compensation: Salary, Benefits, and Intangibles Like "Culture" will help you understand how much to pay and how to find the best benefits for your budget.

Chapter 3—The "Soft" Side: How to Give Feedback and Set Goals for a High Performance Team will guide you through employee engagement, progressive discipline, and termination.

Chapter 4—Legal: All the Stuff You Should Know But Probably Don't covers the fundamentals of U.S. Employment Law, including the Family and Medical Leave Act (FMLA), the Fair Labor Standards Act (FLSA), the Americans with Disabilities Act (ADA), and at-will employment. It also covers risk management, workers compensation, labor relations, and unions.

Chapter 5—Planning for the Future (Assuming You Survive the Now) will help you develop an inclusive culture and plan for growth with strategic workforce planning.

—Marie Carasco
Washington, D.C. Metro Area

—William J. Rothwell
State College, Pennsylvania

Acknowledgments

Writing a book is hard work, don't let anyone tell you any different. This book was no exception.

We, the authors, therefore extend thanks to the many people who helped us throughout this process. That includes our editor, Matt Davis, at the Society for Human Resource Management, and our Advisory Board members:

- Rod Dauphin, MBA—Education Services Director at the Goldman Sachs 10,000 Small Businesses Initiative at LaGuardia Community College
- Don McCandless, MBA—CEO, ConidioTec LLC, former Director of Business Development at Ben Franklin Transformation Services
- Candice Scott, MBA, SHRM-CP—Director, Global Human Resources at International Youth Foundation

We also thank our Advisory Board for reading the book and offering their invaluable comments for improvement. We were guided by their wisdom. While the mistakes are ours, we made our best efforts to follow the advice of our Board. Additional thanks are also extended to those who shared business cases. Understanding your realities will create new possibilities.

Special thanks to Sherwyn Saul, a co-founder of Airnest (acqui-hired by Measure) who created the spark to write this book in the first place.

About the Authors

Marie Carasco, Ph.D., GPHR, SHRM-SCP is the founder and chief social scientist of Talent en Floré LLC, an executive coaching practice supporting individuals interested in personal or professional change (see www.talentenflore.com). She has served as a trusted advisor to C-level leadership teams managing task forces for large-scale global change initiatives and human resources strategy in multiples sectors, including aerospace, engineering, oil and gas, government consulting, and higher education. She is an International Coach Federation Professional Certified Coach (PCC) and member of the NTL Institute for Applied Behavioral Science.

Marie has deep functional expertise in high-potential leader development and appreciative change management using multiple interventions for individual, group, and organization-wide planned change. She teaches masters-level courses in Organizational Behavior, Global Diversity, and Leadership Studies. Her research and professional interests are in leader development, identity and belonging, Organization Development (OD) competencies, HR strategy, and qualitative research methods. She also advises startup and small business leaders on HR strategy.

Marie holds a Ph.D. in Workforce Education and Development with an emphasis in Human Resource Development and Organization Development from The Pennsylvania State University and an Executive MBA in Organizational Behavior and Coaching from the University of Texas at Dallas, Naveen Jindal School of Management. She also holds an undergraduate degree in psychology and a graduate degree in industrial-organizational psychology from CUNY-Brooklyn College.

Marie has authored book chapters in *Evaluating Organization Development: How to Ensure and Sustain the Successful Transformation* (CRC Press, 2017) and *Marketing Organization Development Consulting: A How-To Guide for OD Consultants* (CRC Press, 2017). You can reach her at marie@talentenflore.com.

William J. Rothwell, Ph.D., SPHR, SHRM-SCP, CPLP Fellow is president of Rothwell & Associates, Inc. and Rothwell & Associates, LLC (see www.rothwellandassociates.com). He is also a Professor in the Workforce Education and Development program and the Department of Learning and Performance Systems at The Pennsylvania State University, University Park campus. He has authored, coauthored, edited, or coedited 111 books and almost 200 book chapters and articles.

Before arriving at Penn State in 1993, Rothwell had 20 years of work experience as a director of training, human resources, and organization development in government and business. He has also worked as a consultant for numerous multinational corporations, including Motorola China, General Motors, Ford, and many others. He was the first U.S. citizen named a Certified Training and Development Professional (CTDP) by the Canadian Society for Training and Development in 2004. He earned the American Society for Training and Development's (ASTD) prestigious Distinguished Contribution to Workplace Learning and Performance Award in 2012, and in 2013, ASTD honored him again by naming him as a Certified Professional in Learning and Performance (CPLP) Fellow. In 2014, he was given the Asia-Pacific International Personality Brand Laureate Award (see http://www.thebrandlaureate.com/awards/ibp_bpa.php).

His recent books include *Innovation Leadership* (Routledge, 2018), *Improving Human Performance, 3rd ed.* (Routledge, 2018), *Evaluating Organization Development: How to Ensure and Sustain the Successful Transformation* (CRC Press, 2017), *Marketing Organization Development Consulting: A How-To Guide for OD Consultants* (CRC Press, 2017), *Assessment and Diagnosis for Organization Development: Powerful Tools and Perspectives for the OD Practitioner* (CRC Press, 2017), *Community College Leaders on Workforce Development* (Rowman & Littlefield, 2017), *Organization Development in Practice* (ODNETWORK, 2016), *Mastering the Instructional Design Process, 5th ed.* (Wiley, 2016), *Effective Succession Planning, 5th ed.* (Amacom, 2015), *Practicing Organization Development, 4th ed.* (Wiley, 2015), *The Leader's Daily Role in Talent Management* (McGraw-Hill, 2015), *Beyond Training and Development, 3rd ed.* (HRD Press, 2015), *Career*

Planning and Succession Management, 2nd ed. (Praeger, 2015), *Organization Development Fundamentals: Managing Strategic Change* (ATD Press, 2015), *The Competency Toolkit, 2 vols, 2nd ed.* (HRD Press, 2015), *Creating Engaged Employees: It's Worth the Investment* (ATD Press, 2014), *Optimizing Talent in the Federal Workforce* (Management Concepts, 2014), *Performance Consulting* (Wiley, 2014), the *ASTD Competency Study: The Training and Development Profession Redefined* (ASTD, 2013), *Becoming An Effective Mentoring Leader: Proven Strategies for Building Excellence in Your Organization* (McGraw-Hill, 2013), *Talent Management: A Step-by-Step Action-Oriented Approach Based on Best Practice* (HRD Press, 2012), the edited three-volume *Encyclopedia of Human Resource Management* (Wiley/Pfeiffer, 2012), *Lean But Agile: Rethink Workforce Planning and Gain a True Competitive Advantage* (Amacom, 2012), *Invaluable Knowledge: Securing Your Company's Technical Expertise* (Amacom, 2011), *Competency-Based Training Basics* (ASTD Press, 2010), *Effective Succession Planning: Ensuring Leadership Continuity and Building Talent from Within, 4th ed.* (Amacom, 2010), *Practicing Organization Development, 3rd ed.* (Pfeiffer, 2009), *Basics of Adult Learning* (ASTD, 2009), *HR Transformation* (Davies-Black, 2008), *Working Longer: New Strategies for Managing, Training, and Retaining Older Employees* (Amacom, 2008), and *Cases in Government Succession Planning: Action-Oriented Strategies for Public-Sector Human Capital Management, Workforce Planning, Succession Planning, and Talent Management* (HRD Press, 2008). He can be reached by email at wjr9@psu.edu and by phone at 814-863-2581. He is at 310B Keller Building, University Park, PA 16803.

Introduction

The closer the alignment between the Human Resources (HR) department and an organization's overall business strategy, the better the company's ability to anticipate and respond to customer needs and to maintain a competitive advantage. The benefits of HR strategic planning include the following:

- Avoiding costly and disruptive surprises that interfere with achieving company goals.
- Addressing key issues in a timely manner to avoid crises.
- Promoting employee productivity and overall organizational success.
- Providing a sense of direction to positively affect how work gets done.
- Keeping employees focused on organizational goals.
- Providing a strategic focus to guide training and development initiatives.
- Giving leaders tools to help focus and implement their strategic initiatives.

The Essential HR Guide for Small Businesses and Startups teaches the nuts and bolts of HR and provides:

- A guide to selecting and hiring your first and future hires.
- Simple adaptable tools and templates for performance management and disciplinary action.
- Worksheets to assess your organization's current risks and cultural practices.
- Guidance on risk assessment and plans for continuity of operations.
- Creative approaches to employee benefits.
- Strategies to develop a long-range strategic workforce plan.
- Clarity on how to identify, develop, and promote leaders within the organization.
- Business examples that capture common issues along with questions to consider for your company context.

WHO IS THIS BOOK FOR?

Are you a:

- small business owner?
- small business operations manager?
- manager of finance, operations, and human resources?
- one-person Human Resources department or office manager?
- small human resources team?

...*and you:*

- are responsible for all the HR related work in your company?

This book was designed for companies who may not have the financial resources to invest in a fully staffed HR department. It will help you navigate the decision of *your first hire*, establish and cultivate a culture, and understand *what benefits to offer.* You will also *find tools and resources to manage and measure performance* and ways to *cultivate engagement that encourage team members to stay.* We will help you *understand your legal obligations* such as medical leave and *reasonable accommodations*, how to navigate *labor relations,* and strategies to develop a diverse and inclusive workplace.

SOME IMPORTANT DEFINITIONS

Startup

We define a startup as an early-stage entrepreneurial business that was created to meet an unfilled need in the market. This business is typically owned outright by the founders who provided the initial funding for operational needs. The founders are also the primary staff responsible for doing any and all of the work required in the business.

Small Business

Small businesses are for-profit entities that have been in operation for an average of 5 years and have entered the growth phase. They have a minimum of 4 full-time employees (including the owners) and generate gross revenues in excess of $250,000 to approximately $1 million dollars in annual revenue.

Human Resources

There are two ways to define HR:

1. The actual staff or people that work in the company.
2. A strategic function in the company that helps to manage the people operations to support successful business outcomes. This involves:

   o Administering benefits and compensation
   o Supporting recruitment, onboarding, performance management, and training
   o Strategizing retention, workforce planning, diversity and inclusion, risk management, and employee relations
   o Managing change

HOW TO USE THIS BOOK

The table below is organized by the number of full-time employees (FTE) in a company. We suggest you use it to find what you need as quickly as possible.

Table I.1. Content by Company Size

Book Chapters	Company Size				
	1–10	11–50	51–100	101–150	>150
Chapter 1—Talent: How to Attract, Find, and Train It	√	√	√		
Chapter 2—Compensation: Salary, Benefits, and Intangibles Like "Culture"		√	√	√	√
Chapter 3—The "Soft" Side: How to Give Feedback and Set Goals for a High Performance Team	√	√	√	√	√
Chapter 4—Legal: All the Stuff You Should Know But Probably Don't	√		√	√	√
Chapter 5—Planning for the Future (Assuming You Survive the Now)			√	√	√

Take a Quick Questionnaire

Complete the following questionnaire before you read the book to figure out what you want to get out of *The Essential HR Guide for Small Businesses and Startups* and where you can find what you're looking for—*fast*.

THE QUESTIONNAIRE

Directions

You should spend about 10 minutes on the questions in this questionnaire. Circle Yes (*Y*), Not Applicable (*N/A*), or No (*N*) in the left-hand column opposite each item. Be honest! When you finish, use the instructions at the very end of the questionnaire to score your results. If you'd like, you can then share your responses with others who could help you think about what would be most helpful for you. You can refer to the chapter number in the right-hand column to learn more about a specific question and find more details.

			Does your organization:	
Y	N/A	N	Have a systematic approach to attracting the best people?	1
Y	N/A	N	Have a systematic approach to onboarding and orienting new workers?	1
Y	N/A	N	Have job descriptions that are clear and up-to-date?	1
Y	N/A	N	Possess a clear compensation approach or philosophy?	2
Y	N/A	N	Have a reasonable or conservative approach to benefits?	2
Y	N/A	N	Have a clear sense of pay laws, rules, and regulations affecting your business?	2
Y	N/A	N	Have an effective system to manage performance?	3
Y	N/A	N	Have a system to address corrective action?	3
Y	N/A	N	Have a way to terminate employees that is both legal and fair?	3
Y	N/A	N	Have a sense of how the Family Medical Leave Act (FMLA) affects your organization?	4
Y	N/A	N	Have a sense of how the Fair Labor Standards Act (FLSA) affects your organization?	4
Y	N/A	N	Have a sense of how the Americans with Disabilities Act (ADA) affects your organization?	4
Y	N/A	N	Have a sense of what is meant by an *inclusive* workplace?	5
Y	N/A	N	Have a way to plan for the future workforce needs of the organization?	5
Y	N/A	N	Have a way to clarify the leadership needs of your organization?	5

*Total:*_____

Scoring and Interpreting the Questionnaire

Give yourself **1** point for each Y and **0** for each N or N/A listed above. Total the points from the Y column and place this sum on the line opposite the word *Total*. Then, interpret your score as follows:

Score	
14–15 points	Congratulations! Give your organization a grade of A. Your organization is on the path to having a first-rate HR system.
12–13 points	Give your organization a grade of B. Your organization is making progress in HR but still has room for improvement.
10–11 points	Give your organization a grade of C. Your organization is about average, so your organization should take steps to improve how it manages HR.
8–9 points	Give your organization a grade of D. Your organization is below average. That means you need to play catch up to improve HR.
0–7 points	Give your organization a grade of F. Take immediate steps to improve how your organization manages HR.

For anyone already familiar with the Society for Human Resource Management (SHRM), each chapter will highlight one or more SHRM Knowledge Domain(s) and a corresponding Functional Area(s) part of the SHRM Body of Competency and Knowledge™ (SHRM BoCK™).

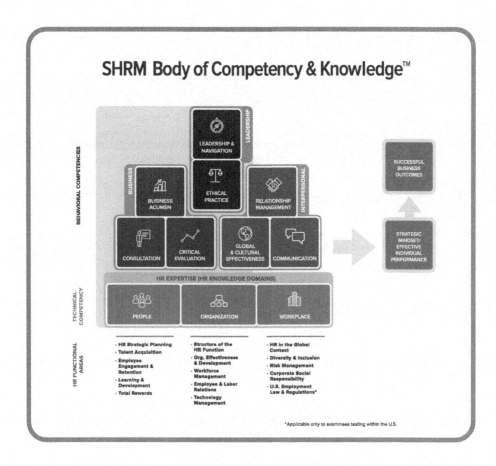

Reprinted with permission. ©Society for Human Resource Management.

About the Advisory Board Members

Rod Dauphin, MBA serves as the director of education services in the Goldman Sachs 10,000 Small Businesses program at LaGuardia Community College. He is responsible for guiding entrepreneurs in the development and implementation of growth strategies for their businesses. Additionally, Dauphin has authored and contributed to the Goldman Sachs 10,000 Small Businesses national curriculum developed by Babson College. Since 2000, Dauphin has immersed himself in entrepreneurship and small business. He has advised well over 500 small businesses in the areas of leadership, marketing, financial management, and company culture.

Don McCandless, MBA is currently the CEO of ConidioTec, a Pennsylvania startup with a revolutionary biopesticide for bed bugs that was launched in October of 2017. Prior to ConidioTec, McCandless worked as the director of business development for the Ben Franklin Technology Partners, providing management assistance to emerging, tech-based start-ups. In addition, he launched and taught the 10-week TechCelerator Boot Camp for Entrepreneurs. Within 5 years, 73 teams graduated, formed 66 companies, received over $26 million in startup funding, and generated $8 million in revenue. For 20 years he held a variety of roles at Restek Corporation, culminating with a five-year tenure as CEO. Somehow, he earned an MBA from the University of Notre Dame and a BS from The Pennsylvania State University.

Candice Scott, MBA has over 15 years of experience in human resources, working for small and large organizations in both the nonprofit and for-profit sectors. The majority of her career has been in building HR functions and departments in small startup IT companies. She holds an MBA with a concentration in Human Resource Management and has a number of HR certifications, including the SHRM-CP. Candice recently accepted a position as the director of global human resources at the International Youth Foundation in Baltimore, MD.

Part I

HR Fundamentals for Startup and Early Stage Businesses

CHAPTER 1

Talent

HOW TO ATTRACT, FIND, AND TRAIN IT

Marie Carasco

QUICK-START GUIDE TO FINDING, ATTRACTING, AND TRAINING TALENT

Chapter One in a Nutshell

Finding the best people for your startup or early stage business should be approached with a proactive strategy that starts with you thinking through short-term (1–3 years) contractual service-based or long-term (5–7 years) skill-based needs.

To do so, you will need to:

- Determine who to hire first
- Write solid job descriptions
- Know when to use a recruiter
- Use job descriptions to guide interviewing and getting people ready to work
- Learn how to make a job offer
- Be deliberate in building your company culture

This chapter focuses on these areas and other related topics.

It Starts When You Start: Building a Company Culture
Business Case and Lessons Learned

Kerry Brodie, the founder and executive director of Emma's Torch, runs a business designed to harness the power of the culinary industry to help refugees build lives in their new communities. As an early-stage non-profit, it has the same operations and challenges of any startup or small business and has been deliberate in building a company culture. After all, your company culture can make or break your business. In chapter three we define culture as "how we do things around here," and the unspoken expectations that guide behavior. These are the most important things you want your employees to demonstrate when they do their work, collaborate with others, or represent your company.

Emma's Torch tends to attract job applicants that are already very *mission-driven*. The people wanting to work there are interested in doing work that is based on a specific business direction, goal, personal belief, value, or way of being. Accordingly, the business has taken deliberate steps in the hiring process and looks for people who align with their mission. In fact, Emma's Torch has a visible version of their *mission statement* hanging on the wall, spelling out the reasons the business exists and how it will get work done. It is a material reminder of their *core values,* or the guiding principles of the company on how they do business. This physical, visible mission statement tends to center the team at Emma's Torch when work becomes stressful or overwhelming. Additionally, one activity the organization has used to help build team culture is a book club. They meet quarterly to discuss the values that arise in the book and how they connect to what they're doing as a company.

Interviewing for Perspective

A candidate applying for a role at Emma's Torch is always asked one question first—"What about your career has led you to the point that you're applying to work at Emma's Torch?" If the applicant does not talk about the mission or why the cause of the business has resonance, it's a nonstarter. This is important because a culture mismatch or bad fit can make getting the job done difficult for the employee and the company. Although the team at Emma's Torch is not expecting a standard response, it is a good start if the applicant demonstrates care for the organization's mission and how the job is the next step in a career.

Another question that is always asked is how the job applicant interacts with others. The question is framed from the perspective of getting in a car: "You're in a car and there's four seats. There's the driver, the navigator, the person who's brought the snacks, and the person who is just enjoying the view." There's no wrong answer, but the team at Emma's Torch always asks every candidate who they are in that car, because they want people who have thought about and can articulate an understanding of "here's how I work." Emma's Torch has found that if a job applicant can explain their best way of working, then they're going to be better at doing their best work.

SHRM Knowledge Domain(s): People
Functional Areas: Talent Acquisition & Retention

Lessons Learned

- Keep reminders about your mission and core values around the office and the worksite to help ground and refocus the team when work becomes challenging.
- Bring everyone together and do team-building activities to strengthen the culture you're wanting to build at your organization.
- Ask interview questions that will help you understand an applicant's career goals and how working for your company fits with those goals.
- Be creative by asking interview questions that will give insight into how someone works and thinks.

FINDING THE BEST PEOPLE

Who wants to work for a startup or early stage business? How do you find those people, especially when your time and recruiting budget are limited? Talented people are everywhere, but the people who want to work for a startup or early stage business are different from the average job applicant. They typically are not averse to risk, are comfortable with long hours, enjoy working with a small team, and welcome multiple responsibilities. We'll elaborate more on these characteristics in chapter two. In the meantime, this chapter will outline reliable startup and early stage business strategies to find the best people. This chapter includes a quick decision tree to use before you begin your search, and information on the importance of linking your talent needs to your overall business strategy, objectives, and mission.

> *Don't despair! If you're an early stage or small business, all these things are important, but we know you don't have a strategy at this point. You can jump to chapter five to learn more about strategic planning connected to hiring for your business needs.*

First things first—what do you need? Most startup and early stage business founders manage and execute projects on their own for two reasons: either they are the experts, or they don't have the cash and/ or financial resources to hire someone else to do their job. However, when the funds are available, the answer to the following question can

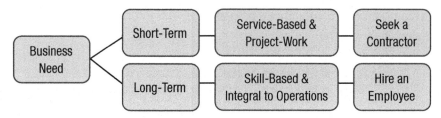

Figure 1.1. Business Needs Decision Tree

help determine the resources you'll need to find the best person. Is this a short-term, service-based need, or a long-term, skill-based need? For many startups and early stage businesses, service-based needs include work performed by lawyers and accountants. They can also include other short-term or one-off projects with a specific end date, like designing a framework, creating a marketing plan, or coding a particular function for an app. Though skill-based needs can be short-term, in this book we define skill-based needs as those a company deems essential to day-to-day operations and are needed on a long-term basis. The distinction is important because short-term, service-based needs are generally contracted out, while long-term, skill-based needs are hired on. See Figure 1.1 to help you figure out your business need for either a contractor or an employee hire.

Employees and independent contractors are two fairly familiar varieties of worker relationships. *Employees* perform work directly for a company on a full or part-time basis. *Independent contractors* provide a service for a company and typically invoice that organization for the tasks performed. The hiring company's only responsibility to the contractor is to provide payment and to submit a 1099 form. A third less common worker relationship is a *contingent worker.* They are employed and paid by a staffing agency. These workers complete tasks for a company; however, the staffing firm covers all their performance evaluations, salaries, and benefits. It's important to understand the legal implications of choosing one of these worker relationships over another. Who could forget Uber, a startup that settled a class action lawsuit for $100 million? The primary issue stemmed from the definition of an independent contractor. It's extremely important that startups and early stage businesses find an experienced attorney to advise the legal implications of choosing and defining one worker relationship over another.

In most states you can call the local bar association and ask for a referral to a lawyer who would be the most helpful for your situation.

When it comes to small business tax filing, classifying a worker properly as an employee or an independent contractor is very important. Getting this wrong will make you liable for employment taxes because the right classification will let you know if you should withhold income tax, Social Security, Medicare, and the unemployment tax. In fact, some business owners wrongly believe that a contract that outlines a worker as an employee or a contractor is enough to define the worker's status. It isn't. Here's the high-level difference:

Employee

- A worker who the business has the right to instruct and to control the work they perform, even if the business chooses not to.
- Paid a regular wage
- Expected to work for an undefined timeframe

Contractor

- Decides what work will be done and how it will be done. The client only has the right to control or direct the result of the work.
- Usually paid a flat fee
- Expected to work for a specific timeframe or project

Visit the IRS' online Small Business and Self-Employed Tax Center for more information on classification.

Your startup or early stage business hiring needs should also be tied to an overall *business strategy,* or where the company is heading based on a desired outcome, objective, and mission. Before you hire or contract someone to join your organization, cross-check your strategic plan (if you have one) to ensure that new talent will help in accomplishing basic goals and objectives. If you haven't thought about a strategic plan, a well-rounded plan should include a big picture approach to staffing that considers long-term needs (three to five years from the present) and not just immediate openings. In other words, business priorities should inform staffing and talent needs. Don't panic if you don't have anything strategic outlined because we'll cover parts of this in chapter five. But, it is important to mention that some startups and early stage businesses pivot and change direction due to market considerations, competition, or innovation. Any change in business direction should trigger an adjustment to the staffing strategy. Even without a pivot, startups should assess the alignment of business priorities on an annual basis at minimum.

Ideally, your company's talent needs should be reviewed periodically in a workforce plan as part of your overall strategic plan (see Figure 1.2 for guidance on getting started). Workforce planning (see chapter five)

Strategic Workforce Plan Key Elements

- Use business goals as the foundation
- Outline short and long-term talent needs
- Evaluate current positions and "what if" scenarios
- Determine hard-to-fill roles
- Identify business critical roles
- Determine skills and knowledge needed to achieve business objectives
- Identify key competencies needed to be successful in your culture and the roles
- Ask if the needs are short-term service-based or long-term skill-based needs
- Understand the impact of your competition on the talent pool
- Establish achievable timelines, milestones
- Assign who will do what
- Create a communications plan
- Define what successful implementation of this plan looks like

Figure 1.2. Key Elements of a Startup or Early Stage Business Strategic Workforce Plan

SHRM Knowledge Domain(s): People
Functional Areas: Talent Acquisition & Retention

brings together the leaders in different divisions of your startup—if there are any. As your business grows, heads of your operations, finance, HR, and marketing departments would be part of that plan. Being clear on your startup's business needs are essential to successfully executing other strategies to find the best people. With that foundation in place, you'll be in a great position to articulate in a job description who you are, what you need, and why future team members should consider applying.

Create a Job Description

Job descriptions are one of those things that nearly every organization uses to communicate talent needs to people outside of the company. They are also useful for illustrating to employees the scope of their work and performance expectations. You can use the following basic checklist to create your job description. For additional references and help with technical jargon on job descriptions, visit the Occupational Information Network (O★NET) OnLine site, a web resource sponsored by the U.S. Department of Labor that provides the public with occupational information. O★NET has over 900 occupations based on the Standard Occupational Classification system, and businesses can use the site for free to quickly develop their job descriptions. Another resource is Insperity, a paid service for creating job posts. You can search by keywords, titles, industries, or categories on their site, www.JobDescription.com, to find your ideal job title. The site also allows you to customize generic content to suit your organization.

Once you have the technical and competency content down, you'll also need to address the WIIFM—"What's in it for me?" At the end of the day, why would anyone want to work at your startup? What do you offer that's unique or interesting? Top talent want to work for great companies, and you'll have to persuade them that you are, in fact, a great company. This boils down to marketing materials (like your web presence) and interpersonal interactions either through social media or customer service experiences. Reputation management is essential. You will need to do a bit of marketing in your job post, while keeping in mind search engine optimization (SEO). The better your SEO, the more likely your post will have greater visibility on job boards. Last, but not least, beware of typographical mistakes and spelling errors, and have your attorney review the post for any red flags or faux pas. See Table 1.1 at the end of this chapter for a basic job description checklist.

You might be wondering if you should include the salary range in the job description. Your decision to include salary or not depends on your compensation philosophy and culture. If you want to adopt a transparent approach to hiring and recruitment, you can include the salary range. This might also help to filter candidates who would not consider the salary, saving you time and resources in the recruiting efforts. We will cover compensation in the section "Deciding What to Pay" in chapter two. In the next section, we outline how to leverage what we consider your treasure trove for finding the best people—your network.

Network Like the Boss You Are

Saying the word "networking" typically raises thoughts of meeting and engaging with new people, an idea that can bring feelings of exhilaration to some and anxiety to others. When it comes to finding the best talent, your networking should begin with people you already know. In this section, we share ways you can leverage your existing network to identify talent for your startup or early stage business. In some large companies, there are referral programs that ask current employees to recommend people for job openings. The idea is that great people know great people, and are unlikely to recommend a slouch that would cast a bad shadow on them. To sweeten the incentive, larger organizations sometimes provide a bonus if the recommended person is hired. Most times, current employees essentially do the first round of filtering, and the organization rewards them for bringing great talent into the company.

Referral programs are an example of leveraging your network in favor of a company. As a leader of a startup, you're now in an influential position in the organization. At this stage, your referral program is informal, without financial rewards, but no less professional. Instead of asking your employees, you will need to reach out to your colleagues, friends, and acquaintances for leads on talented people.

A great start to networking for talent are Small Business Development programs, incubators, or accelerators. Both incubator and accelerator programs have strengths and weaknesses, and no program is exactly alike. However, participants gain access to information and resources that were previously out of reach, including opportunities for meaningful networking. The staff, mentors, and partners working with incubator and accelerator programs have their own contacts, and might know someone who knows someone who could be perfect for the role you're trying to fill.

The Small Business Administration (SBA) provides business guidance and training to entrepreneurs through Small Business Development Centers (SBDCs). Visit the U.S. SBA site at www.sba.gov to find Small Business Development programs and resources for your state. Incubators are programs that provide a space for a startup to develop for a specified period of time. Training and mentorship are also included in the program. Often the startups in an incubator are located in the same physical space funded by the same investor group.

As the name suggests, *startup accelerators* are designed to propel your business forward. They require a few months of time and don't typically provide a dedicated space for the startup. However, accelerators provide training, mentorship, opportunities to refine your pitch, and key resources to help your company prepare for future funding. They invest cash in your business in exchange for a small amount of equity in the company.

Popular tech-based accelerators include Y Combinator, based out of Mountain View, CA, that funded Airbnb and Dropbox. 500 Startups is another accelerator and incubator based in Mountain View, CA, that funds startups in the United States and overseas. F6S, a London-based firm, serves as a one-stop shop for founders. The company posts jobs and is a major first step toward consideration for a number of accelerators and investment funds globally. For more information on F6S, visit www.f6s.com. For a comprehensive list of over 200 seed programs worldwide, visit www.seed-db.com/accelerators. Seed funding is the initial external financial investments raised by a startup enterprise to help get the business to grow. Other good networking sources for startup talent are venture capital (VC) firms. If you've had an opportunity to pitch with a VC firm, or receive funding from one, you ought to mention your startup's strategic hiring need. Asking for a referral is one way of keeping the connection fresh with a purposeful point of contact. VC websites sometimes list open positions in their portfolio companies, and your role could be posted. Using a VC company to post a role is just one way to use a startup-specific platform, and we will discuss other uses of startup-specific platforms in greater detail in the following section. Remember that startups, entrepreneurs, and small business owners should be ready to pitch at any time. Consider preparing a brief and flexible script to use at networking events and for follow-up correspondences (see Table 1.2 at the end of the chapter).

Use Startup-Specific Platforms

No matter where you live or work, there are a few well-known web resources that applicants in given industries use as a go-to place to find vacancies. Keep in mind that anything online can change, so do your digging to see what's current. At the time this book was written, some of the most common sites in the United States were Indeed, LinkUp, SimplyHired, LinkedIn, Facebook, Twitter, CareerBuilder, and Glassdoor. These sites don't quite meet the talent needs of startups and early stage businesses because they tend to be geared toward larger corporate companies. The following platforms are specific to startup and early stage businesses and provide basic to premium services to connect founders with the right talent.

AngelList

One of the few platforms with no middlemen is AngelList, which allows applicants to speak directly to startup founders. No recruiters are allowed. AngelList facilitates a private job search platform where only the companies to which a potential employee applied can see that applicant's job search. Applicants can browse by categories known as job collections, which include drones, breakout companies, female founders, remote, and more. Startup leaders and applicants can also take advantage of the salary and equity data shared upfront before the application process. This information can be sorted by role, location, equity, market, and skills. Creating a profile on AngelList is free, and startups get notified when an applicant indicates interest in a role posted. The site facilitates an introductory email, and discussions are launched from there.

Upwork

This site is the go-to resource for startups and larger organizations looking for budget-friendly, highly qualified freelancers for short-term projects. Here's how it works. You upload a short job description and the freelancer submits a cover letter and link to a profile highlighting specific skills. The site emphasizes personalized recommendations, and you decide who to interview and hire. Payment to freelancers on Upwork is based on either a per-hour or per-project basis through the Upwork payment system (linked via PayPal). Upwork deducts 10% from the freelancer rate. If you don't have time to vet applicants yourself, Upwork has an option to pre-vet applicants for you.

StartupHire

StartupHire is a job search engine for startup career and venture-capital-backed opportunities across the United States. The search options allow applicants to filter by industry, investor, stages, and job function. For a fee, startups posting roles can take advantage of active and passive candidates with startup experience. There are also premium options that include a private recruiting database and social media blasts on Twitter and Facebook. Venture capital investors can take advantage of StartupHire's widget to view career opportunities across a portfolio.

VentureLoop

Supporting venture-backed companies is the niche of VentureLoop, which aims to connect venture capital firms, entrepreneurs, and service providers in job searches. If your startup is associated with any of VentureLoop's 80-plus venture capital clients (found on their "About Us" page), posting job openings is free. Non-clients can expect to pay about $99 per post, many of which can't be found on any other job boards.

Should your business grow to the point of needing help with payroll, benefits, and other related services, VentureLoopHR is the organization's premier outsource HR service for startups.

F6S

If you're looking for a mega database, F6S is a London-based resource that shares more than 12,000 startup programs around the world. The name comes from shortening the six letters between F and S in the word "founders." Listing jobs on F6S is free, and applicants can log on through a Facebook or LinkedIn application programming interface (API), a way of allowing someone to use their log-in credentials from one site to access another site.

Some International Resources

For those living and working outside of the United States, a good starting point is XING, a social network for business professionals. Users can connect to find jobs, new assignments, experts, and collaboration opportunities, mainly in Germany. A similar professional network out of France called Viadeo boasts 40 million members around the world. They have focused development of cultural features for France, Russia, and North Africa. If the idea of managing applicant platforms makes you antsy, then outsourcing your hiring process might be a viable option if you have the money.

Hire a Recruiter or Staffing Firm

When time is a constraint, resources are available, and the roles are critical, you might consider hiring a recruiter or engaging the support of a staffing firm. Performing a simple keyword search on LinkedIn would provide you with a list of recruiters with experience in startups. Understanding your company's needs is essential to maximizing the use of recruiting services, and adequately communicating those needs is equally important. Use the basic job description checklist mentioned earlier in the chapter to capture the skills required for the work, but also spend time describing the culture of the business. Recruiting companies will reach out to *passive candidates* (people not looking for a job right now) and *active candidates* (people looking for a new role now or soon) and screen them before introducing them to you and your team. Depending on the agreement made with the recruiting company or independent recruiter, their pay isn't provided until a candidate is selected and hired. Typically, a percentage (about 20%) of the candidate's salary is the fee. There may also be guarantees made (six months to one year) about how long the candidate remains with your company.

DETERMINING YOUR FIRST HIRE

Not all business owners are clear on who to hire first. In fact, the idea of bringing someone else onboard can be nerve-racking because you don't want to hire the wrong person. Once you've clarified that you really need to hire someone, either because you can't do it yourself anymore, or you or your business partners don't have specific skills that your company needs to get the product or service to market, it's time to open a search for your first employee. Use Table 1.3 at the end of the chapter for a helpful method for thinking through your first hire based on the skillset that is most critical for your business right now, what purpose the job will serve, and how long you'll need that skill for your business.

After completing the first hire evaluations sheet, you should have a baseline understanding of what skillset is most critical, for what purpose, and for how long. A word of caution: if the skillset is critical and is needed for a year or less, revisit Figure 1.1 with the business needs decision tree and reevaluate your short-term needs. You can use the first hire evaluation sheet multiple times to think through the second and third most important skillsets to build and sustain your business for additional hires or training purposes.

The Art of Interviewing

Now that you're clear on the specific skills needed in your next hire, you should prepare for the interview. As a business owner, you should know that candidates are also evaluating you and will think about how you present the company not only during the interview, but also during every interaction, including emails and phone calls. That said, if you're a laid-back business, be true to that culture and don't adopt a corporate approach if that's not how you work. It goes without saying that no matter your business culture, every employee and future employee should be treated with respect and professionalism.

Interviewing can take place over the phone, by video, in person, one-on-one, or in a group. The questions can focus on behaviors, competencies, or specific situations. Most business, no matter the size, will initially screen potential candidates with a short phone call (20–30 minutes). During this call, you should be prepared to introduce yourself, share your role with the company, and also let the candidate know about how long they could expect to be on the call. The art of interviewing begins with preparation. Some baseline questions for a typical phone screen are:

- What interests you about this role?
- What do you know about our company?
- Can you walk me through your resume and why you left each position?
- Tell me about your experience doing _____?
- What are you looking for in terms of salary?

These questions will help gauge the candidate's communication style, interest in the role, and how well their skills fit the position. After this call, you can determine if having a video or face-to-face interview makes sense.

In-person interviews tend to be about an hour and can involve anywhere from 10–12 questions. However, you'll want to leave about 10 minutes for the candidate to ask you questions at the end. This interview is your opportunity to understand if the person applying to your company has the skills, experience, and potential to do the work that you need. *Behavior*, *competency*, and *situation-based* questions will be your best options for examples of when and how the candidate used specific skills. These questions are typically worded in ways that are similar to:

- Tell me about a time when you _____?
- We have _____ situation, how would you handle _____?
- Describe how you _____?

SHRM Knowledge Domain(s): People
Functional Areas: Talent Acquisition & Retention

You'll notice that these are open-ended questions that require the candidate to share in detail their approach to a past or future event. Avoid asking closed-ended questions that could have "yes" or "no" answers—they won't help you understand how the person got things done.

There are questions that should never be asked. Avoid questions about an applicant's marital status, children, pregnancy status, age, gender identity, prescription drug use, disability, national origin, religion, race, color, clubs, societies, lodge memberships, or health status. The U.S. government requires employers to verify identity and employment eligibility of new hires through the Employment Eligibility Verification (I-9) Form. However, while you can ask if the person is authorized to work for any employer in the U.S., questions about a person's citizenship should not be asked before extending an offer. Finally, be careful with pre-employment tests. As stated by the U.S. Equal Employment Opportunity Commission (EEOC), "If an employer requires job applicants to take a test, the test must be necessary and related to the job and the employer may not exclude people of a particular race, color, religion, sex (including gender identity, sexual orientation, and pregnancy), national origin, or individuals with disabilities. In addition, the employer may not use a test that excludes applicants age 40 or older if the test is not based on a reasonable factor other than age." For more information, visit the EEOC website and search for prohibited employment policies and practices. You can also visit the U.S. Department of Labor website under the topic "Hiring" for additional resources.[1]

PICKING THE BEST PERSON FOR THE JOB

There's a certain confidence that comes with having a strong understanding of what your business needs. Even with that clarity, choosing the best person for the job can be challenging. You might be tempted to go with your gut, but gut feelings are a shaky foundation to build your business. The decision is better when based on the facts: candidate experience, skills, and potential. How are those factors connected to your business needs? If there's a match, then the next logical step is extending an offer that is contingent on successful completion of reference checks, a background check, and a drug screening. Don't be tempted to skip these screenings. They're not a guarantee, but can at least provide important information about some potential risks associated with hiring someone.

Before You Make an Offer

There are a several legal requirements you'll want to have in place before you hire anyone. If you're unable to do so, you're not ready to hire. Use the checklist in Table 1.4 at the end of the chapter as a guide.

Making the Offer

Extending a job offer is an exciting part of the hiring process. Chapter two outlines in detail how to research and benchmark salary information. Once you have a couple of people in mind that you believe would be a good fit for your business, it's a common practice to make a verbal offer by phone to your first pick. A verbal offer covers the high-level terms of employment, such as the title, salary, and a proposed start date. If you have a trusted business partner or legal team, think about rehearsing the presentation of the offer with them to get feedback on your approach. See the verbal offer script in Table 1.5 at the end of the chapter to get started.

There are three possible responses from the applicant to your offer: they accept it right away, ask for more time to think it over, or turn it down. If they ask for more time, let them know that's perfectly fine and share any time constraints you have so they know when to circle back to you. If the offer is turned down, express your regret and ask if they'd mind sharing why. Depending on the response they provide, you may or may not have the ability to get the offer closer to what they are looking for. Finally, if they accept, express your excitement, welcome them to the team, and follow-up with a written offer letter. The offer letter should be reviewed by your legal counsel and typically includes:

- The job title
- A start date
- Employment status (full-time, part-time, or contractor/project) and shift (if applicable)

- A statement that employment is at will (except in Montana)
- Salary and pay periods
- Benefits information (including paid time off information)
- Terms of employment, such as background checks and drug screening
- Whom to contact for questions
- Signature and date

THE VALUE AND CULTIVATION OF CULTURE

If you were asked to describe your company culture, could you do it? And should you care? Every company has a culture, whether they know how to describe it or not. In fact, founders of businesses are the most influential in shaping a company culture. Great companies have healthy cultures, which can contribute to profitability. If the culture shows any sign of being anything but positive, you could very likely trace the issues back to the top. Earlier in the chapter, we defined culture as the unspoken expectations that guide behaviors and the way things are done. Cultures are understood through experience and observation, not written statements or marketing materials. In other words, your employees are more likely to do what they see. For example, if your company claims to value work-life balance but new team members see employees working 12-hour days, they will more than likely feel compelled to put in the same number of hours regardless of any statements around work-life balance. Building a healthy culture starts by consistently modeling healthy behaviors related to decision making, communication, hiring, rewards and recognition, and termination. It also requires courage to make difficult decisions like holding team members accountable for things like cutting corners, abrasive behavior, or doing things unethically.

Creating a culture is a lot easier than changing it, and being clear on the type of culture you'd like to create will help in outlining the best ways to orient new hires to your company. Table 1.6 has some basic steps and exploration questions to help in creating a healthy culture.

Orienting New Hires to Your Company

Believe it or not, new hire orientation begins before the first day on the job. Prospective candidates would be wise to pay careful attention to every point of contact made with your business, because these contact points are strong indicators of what to expect on the job. That said, once your new employee has agreed to a start date, the work begins in developing a positive and welcoming experience that will help them feel good about their decision to work for you, and also help them prepare to hit the ground running. If the new hire will be working in a physical office space, prepare that space with supplies, a welcome note, and some swag like a mug, pen, or shirt with the company logo. Both virtual and non-virtual team members should also receive a welcome email from the management team. This email should also contain a list of links to relevant resources.

You can save a few trees and a lot of time by sending new hire paperwork electronically using email and DocuSign. You can also leverage an online platform like Onboardia, which provides new hires with a central place to complete forms, trainings, and surveys. The first official day on the job might include finalizing paperwork like the I-9, several introduction meetings with a few key team members, and a tour of the location (if applicable). There should also be a meeting with the new hire's manager to talk generally about the company culture and policies, goals, performance management, the vision for the role, and expectations for the first week. It would be helpful to have both the manager and new hire share preferred communication and work styles. The new hire should be given guidance on where to find resources and whom to ask for help. Some companies plan for a lunch with the new hire and the other team members on the first day, which is a nice way to make connections early on. During the first month, there should be at least one meeting scheduled every week to touch base on the work and the transition into the company. Plan to schedule a meeting at the end of the month for the first three months to understand what is working well and what would allow things to work even better.

SHRM Knowledge Domain(s): People
Functional Areas: Talent Acquisition & Retention

JOB TITLES MAKE A DIFFERENCE

Talent Business Case and Lessons Learned

Alan, the CEO of a startup in the southwest region of the United States, posted a job on AngelList for a director of human resources. The job description was very brief, but included a salary range and possible equity. Candidates started pouring in, and the post was attracting people with a lot of experience in HR. During an interview with a mid-career HR professional, Alan shared what he wanted to accomplish with this job. He was lucky enough to get some direct feedback during the interview from the applicant, who told him that the job description as it was didn't capture what his company needed. He was advised to edit its description to reflect a lower level of experience and skills based on what his business needed now, rather than what he envisioned would be needed in the future. The role was changed to an HR generalist with responsibility for administration and more junior-level support. Without the feedback directly from a candidate, Alan might not have considered the true significance of the job title in his AngelList post. Inflated or inaccurate titles not only lead to disappointment, but also could potentially damage the reputation of your business.

RESOURCES, TEMPLATES, AND TOOLS FOR MANAGING TALENT
(Items in italics can be found in the appendix.)

Recruiting and Talent Acquisition
Hiring Checklist

Job Offers
Job Offer Checklist
Conditional Job Offer Template
Unconditional Job Offer Template
Temporary Position Job Offer Template

Interview Questions
Telephone Interview Pre-Screening Form

SHRM Knowledge Domain(s): People
Functional Areas: Talent Acquisition & Retention

U.S. Equal Employment Opportunity Commission, "Prohibited
Employment Policies and Practices," https://www.eeoc.gov/laws/
practices/

Hiring the Right Employee
Robert J. Grossman, "Hiring to Fit the Culture," *HR Magazine*,
February 2, 2009, https://www.shrm.org/hr-today/news/
hr-magazine/Pages/0209grossman.aspx
Background Check Form (Phone)
Background Check Request by Mail

Onboarding
Arlene S. Hirsch, "Designing and Implementing an Effective
Onboarding Strategy," https://www.shrm.org/resourcesandtools/
hr-topics/talent-acquisition/pages/designing-and-implementing-
an-effective-onboarding-strategy.aspx
Roy Mauer, "New Employee Onboarding Guide," *SHRM Online*,
https://www.shrm.org/resourcesandtools/hr-topics/talent-
acquisition/pages/new-employee-onboarding-guide.aspx

ADDITIONAL TOOLS

Table 1.1. Basic Job Description Checklist

Use the checklist below to draft your job description. In the left-hand column is the specific element or high-level category in the job description. The right-hand column gives details about each element that you need to include as you write the description.

Element	General Content
Job Title	Define the role in a few words, or at most, as a short sentence describing the work needed.
Company Description	Summarize your company's focus, products, mission, etc. Don't forget to note something unique or interesting.
Job Details	Describe the key duties and responsibilities of the project or role and what you expect to be done.
Qualifications/ Skills	Mention any special requirements or experience needed for the project.
How to Apply	Inform the applicant how to apply and by when.

© Copyright 2020 by Marie Carasco

SHRM Knowledge Domain(s): People
Functional Areas: Talent Acquisition & Retention

Table 1.2. Basic Script to Network for Talent

Use the following scripts when you are networking to find talent for your company. The script in the left-hand column is for people you know well, while the script in the right-hand column is for people you don't know well. Both scripts can be used for a face-to-face conversation, an email, or a direct message.

For People You Know Well	For People You Don't Know Well
Tell them…	Tell them…
• Why you are contacting them (omit if face-to-face) • The talent you need • Business goal tied to your talent need • How they can help	• Your name • How you met • Why you are contacting them (omit if face-to-face) • What your company does • The talent you need • Business goal tied to your talent need • How they can help

Email/Direct Message Example	Face-to-face "Conversational" Example
Hi Chuck, How are you and the family doing? It was nice catching up with you last month. I am reaching out to see if you know anyone that might be a good fit for a new role we have at UpTheAnty. We're looking for a part-time SEO Analyst to improve our marketing and promotion efforts in the Bay Area. If you know anyone, I'd be interested in setting up a meeting. Thanks in advance. Jackie	Hi! [While extending your hand for a handshake] We met at the Tech Stars event in April. I'm Jackie, one of the cofounders of UpTheAnty. We help people find lost coins. I am glad to connect with you again because our company is looking to hire a part-time SEO Analyst to improve our marketing and promotion efforts in the Bay Area. If you know anyone that might be interested please let me know. Here's my card…

Table 1.3. First Hire Evaluation Sheet

To identify your company's high-level business need, write your answers to the questions on the left and choose which box on the right makes the most sense at this time.		
What specific skillset is missing that is *the most critical* to sustain or build in the business at this time?	Technical ☐	Other ☐
In what ways will that skillset help the business?	Growth ☐	Other ☐
Timing and Time Commitments		
How soon will this skillset be integrated into the team?	>6 mos. ☐	<6 mos. ☐
How often will the work connected to this skillset occur? (daily, weekly, monthly, etc.)	Frequently ☐	Infrequently ☐
Note: Frequent skillset use may lead to a full-time hire, versus part-time for infrequent use.	Full-time Hire	Part-time Hire
How long do we expect this skillset to be needed? (one year , five years, for the life of the company, etc.)	Years ☐	Forever ☐

© *Copyright 2020 by Marie Carasco*

Table 1.4. Basic Business Legal Requirements Before Extending an Offer

Read the legal requirement on the left and the associated description on the right, then check either the "Yes" or "No" box to determine if your company has met the basic legal requirement needed before extending a job offer.

Legal Requirement	Description	Yes	No
Employer Identification Number (EIN)	The IRS requires that your company have an EIN number for tax returns. Visit www.irs.gov.	☐	☐
Register with the state labor department	Each state has an unemployment fund that employers pay into. Your state may also require a state or local ID number. Visit the U.S Department of Labor State Labor Office page at https://www.dol.gov/whd/contacts/state_of.htm.	☐	☐

Legal Requirement	Description	Yes	No
Workers' Compensation	Most states require workers' compensation to cover on-the-job accidents, with an exception for very small companies.	☐	☐
Employee W-4 forms	New employees are required to complete a W-4 form for tax withholdings. Download on www.irs.gov.	☐	☐
Report to state's new hire reporting agency	Each state has a requirement that employers report new employees for the purpose of child support. Visit www.acf.hhs.gov for more information.	☐	☐
Establish a payroll system to withhold taxes for the IRS	Employers need to withhold a portion of each employee's income to send to the IRS. These include Medicare and Social Security. Visit www.irs.gov and review Publication 15, Circular E, Employer's Tax Guide for more information. Payroll taxes are typically due quarterly and annually.	☐	☐
Form I-9, Employment Eligibility Verification	The United States Citizenship and Immigration Services requires proof of eligibility to work in the United States. Each employee needs to have a separate I-9 folder that should be kept for three years and is available for inspection or auditing. Visit www.uscis.gov for forms and information.	☐	☐
Form 940	Every year, employers are required to file Form 940 to report federal unemployment tax at $1,500 or more in a quarter of a year for an employee who worked 20 or more different weeks of the year. Visit www.irs.gov for more information.	☐	☐
Post Department of Labor notices	The Department of Labor and your state have specific posters that are required to be made available and visible to employees about workers' rights. Visit www.dol.gov/elaws/posters.htm for more information.	☐	☐

Legal Requirement	Description	Yes	No
Implement workplace safety standards	The Occupational Safety and Health Act requires employers to have established standards that allow for a hazard-free workplace. Employers should keep safety records, provide adequate training to employees so work can be performed safely, and inform the government if there are serious workplace accidents. Visit the Occupational Safety and Health Administration at www.osha.gov for additional guidance.	☐	☐
Create employee records filing system	Each new hire should have their own personnel file that contains: • Employee's full name and Social Security number • Job application • Offer letter, including pay rate, pay frequency, and FLSA status • W-4 form • I-9 (in a separate file) • Benefits sign-up forms • Mailing address and zip code • Birth date, if the employee is younger than 19 years old • Sex and occupation	☐	☐

© Copyright 2020 by Marie Carasco

Table 1.5. Verbal Offer Script

Verbal Offer Script
Hi [candidate name]: This is [your name] calling from [your company name]. Is this a good time to talk? I'm calling about the [position name] and wanted to let you know that [I or we] felt you'd be a great fit with [your company name]. I'm excited at the possibility of you joining our team and would like to extend an offer to you for the [position name] starting at [salary]. We also have [other benefits]. We're working on the full details of the offer, but I wanted to reach out to you and get your thoughts.

© Copyright 2020 by Marie Carasco

SHRM Knowledge Domain(s): People
Functional Areas: Talent Acquisition & Retention

Table 1.6. Steps to Create a Healthy Culture

Think about the most important things you want your employees to demonstrate when they represent your company, then answer the following questions to help you develop a healthy culture.

Explore Core Values

What are the things you stand for and believe in (principles) that you'd like to see in others who work with you?

How would those principles be observed or experienced by the staff at your company?

Lead by Example

What are you doing now that you know needs to change to create a healthier work environment?

What could you do more of that would encourage your team to take corrective actions?

Pursue Equity

Are there places where you have shown favoritism to one person over another? If so, to whom and why?

Where can you create a more balanced approach to inclusion? (e.g. decision-making, delegation, etc.)

Identify Culture Champions

Who in the company is consistently demonstrating the company culture you want to see in others?

SHRM Knowledge Domain(s): People
Functional Areas: Talent Acquisition & Retention

What questions might you ask in an interview to identify someone that would fit the culture you want to build? (Hint: consider core values)

Caution: Your questions should not discriminate.

Create Rituals

What daily, weekly, monthly, and yearly activities can be done to reinforce the desired culture?

How will you capture and respond to employee feedback?

© *Copyright 2020 by Marie Carasco*

REFERENCES

U.S. Equal Employment Opportunity Commission. "Prohibited Employment Policies/Practices." Accessed March 29, 2019. https:// www.eeoc.gov/laws/practices/.

ENDNOTES

1. "Prohibited Employment Policies/Practices," U.S. Equal Employment Opportunity Commission, accessed March 29, 2019, https://www.eeoc.gov/laws/practices/.

Compensation

SALARY, BENEFITS, AND INTANGIBLES LIKE "CULTURE"

Marie Carasco

QUICK-START GUIDE TO COMPENSATION, BENEFITS, AND CULTURE
Chapter Two in a Nutshell

Deciding what to pay and what benefits to offer is a very important aspect of your startup, early stage business, or small business recruitment strategy. A carefully planned comprehensive compensation approach will be key to attracting talented people to grow with your organization.

To do so, you will need to:

- Understand the nuts and bolts in a compensation philosophy
- Learn the basic/minimum benefits required by law in the United States
- Navigate a conservative approach to benefits tied to funding levels
- Benchmark compensation approaches by industry and region
- Consider equity to attract, motivate, and retain key talent
- Leverage creativity in designing compensation and benefits that reflect the needs and wants of current and future employees

This chapter focuses on these areas and other related topics.

Equity vs. Bonuses for Retention:
Benefits Business Case and Lessons Learned

A manufacturing company in the Northeast had been very successful and wanted to share the wealth with the team. They didn't have some of the traditional benefits like a 401k plan, so the owner decided to give his employees quarterly bonuses, and they loved it. After a few years, the owner decided to sell the company and stay on as the president. The new owner had another company that he ran differently, and he wanted to run the newly acquired company in the same way. He didn't like the idea of giving bonuses as a benefit in this company and decided to offer equity instead, believing that equity would encourage people to stay with the company. *Equity* represents ownership in a company. He thought that because employees knew how successful the company had been, they would recognize how valuable the equity shares would be when the business eventually went public. The new owner gave the employees two options. The first option was to swap the bonus money for the same amount of equity shares. For example, if an employee got a $10,000 bonus each year, that employee could swap out the bonus and get 10,000 equity shares, making the offer $1 per share. The second option was to build that bonus amount into their base salary.

The Results and the Impact

Most of the employees, especially the younger, lower-level staff, opted to roll the bonus into their base salary instead of taking the equity, and a few highly compensated staff took the equity. If retention was the goal, it backfired. Not too long after the changes were made, a large number of the staff resigned. On their way out, these soon-to-be former staff members were given the option to buy equity shares. However, without knowing if or when the company would ever go public, the offer to buy shares wasn't attractive. For those without a clear understanding of the long game in equity buying, it can seem like a risky and expensive investment that the highly compensated staff chose on their way out.

The use of equity shares as a retention tool evolved into a recruiting tool in this company. Within the first year of the change from bonuses to equity, new hires got an offer letter basically saying that they have the potential to acquire equity shares after a year of service. After that year, the company removed the equity option from offer letters because it wasn't a helpful recruiting tool for certain positions, specifically lower-level roles that required a few years of experience, technical roles, and roles requiring non-management professionals. Many of these employees simply didn't understand the benefit and there wasn't much time available to explain it to them. Equity shares were then only offered to highly compensated C-levels or director-level roles, or people that came in the door with an understanding of equity shares as a benefit.

Lessons Learned

For this company, bonuses were a better retention tool than equity shares for a majority of the employees. It became clear that "cash" compensation was more important to staff with lower salaries than those being paid high wages. The change from bonuses to equity also appeared to favor

SHRM Knowledge Domain(s): People
Functional Areas: Total Rewards

those with high wages since they were the ones that were able to afford to buy equity shares if they resigned.

- Design your approach to benefits thinking about the real impact of staff with high and low wages.
- Understand what motivates your employees to stay and what benefits keep them there.
- Use caution when thinking about copying another company's benefit offerings.
- Explain equity as a benefit to everyone that it's offered to.

DECIDING WHAT TO PAY

As the old saying goes, "you get what you pay for." So what should you pay? There's a lot of information out there about setting up a traditional compensation and benefits approach. Though it's great to keep in mind and to build toward, it's not very helpful when starting out. The thing that traditional compensation structures have in common with a startup or early stage business is a compensation philosophy. Every company has one, whether or not they admit it. It's the foundation that a company will rely on when thinking about why it makes the pay choices it does and how to consistently approach pay equity in the organization. Depending on factors such as the economic conditions, company size, and success of the approach, a compensation philosophy can change to meet current needs. It can also change at the whim of the executive team.

Case in point: in 2015, Dan Price, CEO of Gravity Payments, a Seattle-based credit card processing company, increased the minimum salary of all his staff to $70,000 per year. This move created more than a few ripples in the media, especially because he cut his own million-dollar compensation to help in covering the cost. The move was motivated in part by Price reading a study that linked earning extra income to improvements in happiness. This baseline belief shifted the organization's compensation philosophy to one that gave everyone the same salary no matter the role. The move was not without controversy and even legal action from a stakeholder in the company. Some employees quit with the sentiment that the raise wasn't fair to higher wage earners. Needless to say, the world is well aware of the compensation philosophy at Gravity Payments.

Nuts and Bolts in a Startup or Early Stage Business Compensation Philosophy
Having the right compensation philosophy will help guide your startup or early stage business through the various levels of growth and investment. In developing your company's compensation philosophy, culture is king. What kind of company do you want to be? Will you be the kind of company that will pay people as little as possible, or one that will pay a fair wage based on the market and your budget constraints? Will you be transparent with salary information or not? Paired with your mission statement, a well-formed compensation philosophy can help your organization connect to your business strategy.

Step One: Align with Culture
- What does our approach to compensation say about us? Do we care?
- What exactly will be shared and with whom?

Step Two: Connect to Business Strategy
- How will our approach to compensation move us toward our business goals?
- What are our competitors doing?
- What can we afford?

If your business has the time and interest in creating a compensation strategy and salary structure from scratch, this next section will show you a very detailed and formal way on how to do it. Otherwise, you can skip this section.

A general example of a compensation philosophy has the following sections: objectives, stakeholder alignment, ethics and culture, risk management, regulatory guidance, and attract and retain talent. When developing your startup or early stage business compensation philosophy, much like your mission statement, pay attention to your choice of words.

SHRM Knowledge Domain(s): People
Functional Areas: Total Rewards

After creating a philosophy, compensation structures can either be built from scratch or you can purchase existing structures for several hundred dollars from any number of consulting firms, including Mercer, Willis Towers Watson, and the Society for Human Resource Management (who get their data from Willis Towers Watson). Organizations like PayScale (www.payscale.com) and Salary.com (www.salary.com) also offer the option of purchasing salary survey data. These organizations can also help you develop a salary structure. But if you want a fast and free option, google for salary information and sites. PayScale, Salary.com, Indeed, and Glassdoor can all be helpful. Search for a job title, then input the city or zip code for the job and any other information you have about the experience needed. These sites will generate a range of salaries from highest to lowest based on the information you provided. This is a great baseline starting point you can use for free.

Building a Comp Structure from Scratch

The Society for Human Resource Management provides the following steps for building a compensation structure from scratch:

- **Step 1:** Determine the organization's compensation philosophy (which we just went over)
- **Step 2:** Conduct a job analysis
  - o Document and analyze information about the job to determine the activities and responsibilities it includes, its relative importance to other jobs, the qualifications necessary for performing the job, and the conditions under which the work is performed.
  - o This can be done by observing employees, conducting surveys, interviewing employees doing the job, or using a combination of these methods. The end result of a job analysis is a clearly defined job description.
- **Step 3:** Group into job families
  - o Determine whether to group the jobs into separate job families or have one pay grade system for all positions throughout the organization.

SHRM Knowledge Domain(s): People
Functional Areas: Total Rewards

o For example, an organization may have an administrative job family, technical job family, management job family, and executive job family.
- **Step 4:** Rank positions using one of the following job evaluation methods
  o Ranking jobs based on their duties and responsibilities—not the people in them—to demonstrate the relative worth and level of responsibility between all the positions.
    » *Point method.* Factors are qualities of a job that are common to many fields of work, such as skill required, effort, or working conditions. Each factor is assigned a weight, or points, according to how much of that particular factor is present in the job. Simply stated, the more points assigned to a job, the more worth the job has to the organization.
    » *Ranking method.* This ranking method is less rigorous and is often used in smaller organizations that have fewer jobs to compare. It's a much more simplistic approach to ranking the value or worth of each job in comparison to other jobs within the same job family. Job ranking places jobs in a hierarchy of their value to the company. This method is an estimated approach rather than a formal calculation as described in the point factor method.
- **Step 5:** Conduct market research (which we outlined earlier in the chapter)
- **Step 6:** Create job grades
  o Job grades are groupings of positions with similar worth.
  o A startup, early stage business, or small organization may have only three or four pay grades.
  o Organizations can either use their job evaluation data to group positions into job grades or use their market data to band together positions based on similar salary survey data.
- **Step 7:** Create a salary range based on research
  o There is no hard and fast rule for creating salary ranges.
  o Employers should note the range of pay in the salary surveys and other information that may be relevant when establishing an average salary.

SHRM Knowledge Domain(s): People
Functional Areas: Total Rewards

o For each pay grade, an organization will need to establish minimum, midpoint, and maximum pay ranges.

o Employers often consider their midpoint of a salary range to be somewhere between the 25th and 75th percentile.

o Some employers will use the 50th percentile, median, mean, or mode if they want to meet the market. If a company's philosophy is to lead the market, the salary point will be above the 50th percentile for most positions.

o A simple way to establish a proposed midpoint is to average the market data between the different positions grouped in a grade.

o A traditional salary range is commonly 30–40 percent.

» The formulas for a 30 percent range using the midpoint as the base are:

Maximum = Midpoint × 1.15
Minimum = Midpoint × 0.85

» The formulas for a 40 percent range when the midpoint is known are:

Maximum = Midpoint × 1.20
Minimum = Midpoint × 0.80

o Pay grade ranges will usually overlap. The more overlap, the more cost-effective it will be for career progression; less overlap will require a larger pay increase for internal promotions.

o Each job family can have its own pay grades and pay ranges that are established independently from other job families.

• **Step 8:** Determine how to address salaries not within range

o At this stage in the process, an organization can look at what it is paying its employees in comparison to the data it has collected and the proposed salary grades and ranges for positions.

o The organization may need to make some adjustments, but overall the employer can rely on market data and its pay philosophy to set these ranges.

Table 2.1. Point Method Example

Factors	Job Title		
	Machine Operator I (points)	Machine Operator II (points)	Machine Operator III (points)
Skill (Max Pts 50)	10	30	50
Education (Max Pts 25)	5	5	10
Working Conditions (Max Pts 10)	5	5	5
Independent Judgment (Max Pts 15)	3	8	15
Total Points (Max Pts 100)	23	48	80

Reprinted with permission. © Society for Human Resource Management.

Table 2.2. Proposed Ranges Examples

Proposed Ranges	Min	Mid	Max
Grade I	$11.48	$13.50	$15.53
Maintenance I		(market salary = $13.00)	
Administrative Asst.		(market salary = $14.00)	
Grade II	$15.09	$17.75	$20.41
Mechanic I		(market salary = $17.50)	
Machinist		(market salary = $18.00)	

Reprinted with permission. © Society for Human Resource Management.

Creating a compensation structure from scratch takes time that most early stage businesses don't have. We thought you should have it as a reference so when it makes sense, you can always come back to this section.

SHRM Knowledge Domain(s): People
Functional Areas: Total Rewards

Reality Checks

It doesn't make sense to compare your startup or early stage business to Fortune 500 organizations. The resources those companies have toward employee benefits can't be matched by a startup or early stage business, especially not in the beginning. That said, if the cash compensation is too low, it will inhibit your company's ability to attract good talent, and unrealistically high cash compensation might turn off potential investors and alternative funders, like banks. There is a balance that startup and early stage business organizations can achieve and it begins with taking advantage of the agility and flexibility available in customizing your approach to employee benefits. One thing is certain—most startup or early stage businesses are highly creative. The innovation that founded your company should also drive your thoughts around total compensation. This means thinking beyond base salary and attracting the best people without going broke. The fact of the matter is, funding and administering benefits programs is expensive. Taking a conservative approach toward benefits offerings, from basic to comprehensive, is an excellent strategy that should be based on your business's profitability. See Figure 2.1 for guidance on how to take a conservative approach to benefits based on your funding levels.

Give 'em What They Want and What the Law Requires

There are many organizations currently offering costly benefits that most employees don't want and won't use. To avoid this, ask your incoming team members at any point in your growth cycle what they would like to see reflected in the benefits program. This will be especially valuable for your company when it moves toward more moderate and comprehensive benefits offerings. Depending on the size of your startup or early stage business, you won't have a choice when it comes to certain benefits. For example, healthcare must be provided to full-time employees by companies with 51 or more employees. The Affordable Care Act, passed in

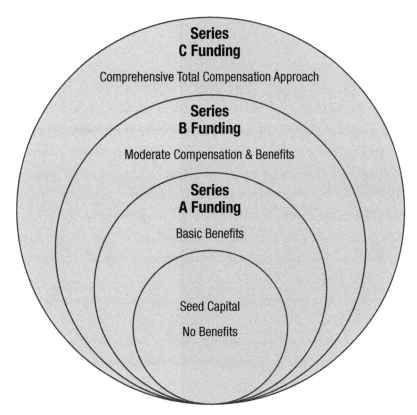

Series C Funding ($10sM-$100sM)—Mature businesses at this state of funding can expect investors primarily from investment banks, private equity firms and large venture capital organizations. Initial Public Offering (IPO) and acquisition by a larger company are often the goal.

Series B Funding ($6M-$10M)—This level of funding is more common in the United States than in Europe, and startups at this stage of investment are interested in scaling.

Series A Funding ($2M-5M)—Startups receiving this level of investment have an established market and product. Investment typically comes from venture capital firms that can take 15% to 30% ownership.

Seed Capital (Up to $1M)—Funds from this level of investment allow a startup to find and build a product to market. Sources include accelerator programs, single angel investors, syndicate investing (angels co-investing), and crowd-funding.

Figure 2.1. Benefits Levels Based on Funding

2010, added some additional requirements (these can be found at www. irs.gov):

> Under the Affordable Care Act's employer shared responsibility provisions, certain employers (called applicable large employers or ALEs) must either offer minimum essential coverage that is "affordable" and that provides "minimum value" to their full-time employees (and their dependents), or potentially make an employer shared responsibility payment to the IRS. The employer shared responsibility provisions are sometimes referred to as "the employer mandate" or "the pay or play provisions." The vast majority of employers will fall below the ALE threshold number of employees and, therefore, will not be subject to the employer shared responsibility provisions [IRS].[1]

Given that there are business tax implications for your startup or early stage business, it's best to discuss the Affordable Care Act and any other potential benefits offerings with your tax advisor before taking any actions. Ask your local small business development center for guidance on finding the right tax person. Keeping these legal requirements in mind, the early stage of developing your benefits offering provides an excellent opportunity to tailor your company's approach to individual employee needs. See Figure 2.2 for the six basic benefits required by law.

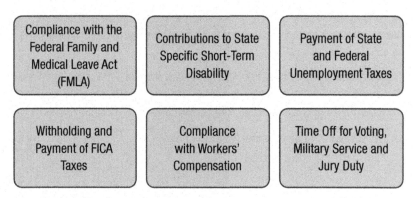

Figure 2.2. Six Basic Benefits Required by U.S. Law

SHRM Knowledge Domain(s): People
Functional Areas: Total Rewards

Don't Ignore Your Competition or Trends in the Sector

People that want to work for a startup or early stage business typically have a number of decent choices. The benefits your organization offers could be their deciding factor and, therefore, a competitive advantage. Bear in mind that there are regional and industry-specific trends when it comes to what is offered as compensation and benefits. Health, wellness, and free food perks appear to be the most common. Larger, more established companies like Netflix offer up to a year of paid leave for new parents of both genders, and they can take time off as needed. Airbnb gives employees an annual stipend of $2,000 for travel anywhere in the world if they stay at an Airbnb site. Twitter offers onsite acupuncture and improv classes, and Google has an incredible benefit that is given to surviving partners of deceased employees—half of their salary for 10 years. Those are typical offerings for Silicon Valley, and although you don't have to try to give the same kind of benefits, a lot of employees have become accustomed to seeing standard benefits offerings.

Common standard benefits offerings are 401(k) plans, vacation time, bonuses, and healthcare. If your startup or early stage business isn't ready to carry those costs, you need to get creative. For example, your company might develop a 401(k) plan at series B funding, take on the administrative costs, but not provide a matching provision right away. Startup or early stage businesses need to be familiar with the tax codes that will best support compensation decisions. For example, deferring taxable income and deductions should be discussed with your tax attorney. Startup or early stage businesses are not required to provide retirement plans, life insurance, paid vacation, or holidays; however, some companies choose to offer these benefits because they are a basic offering by many organizations. It is easier to start small and scale up as your business grows.

CAUTIOUSLY CONSIDER EQUITY

A common expectation in working for a startup or early stage business, especially in the early stages, is to receive equity, or ownership in your company. For cash strapped businesses, equity is major leverage. Equity can be a valuable compensation equalizer that connects a potential employee's market value and the startup or early stage business's cash limitations. Generally, early hires and executives could be granted one to two percent of the total shares in the organization. Employees that took the risk to join your company could have a great return in the long term because they are often able to buy exercisable shares at a large discount, sometimes 10 to one, and not taxed until exercised. There is a chance that the organization may not be successful, and to have an employee wait four years to have the options vest might seem like an eternity. However, if the startup or early stage business is highly successful, these early employees could become rich.

Supplementing cash compensation with stock is only as valuable as it is understood. Future employees need to be educated about what the stocks represent and what they could mean without overselling. Facebook developed a guide to understanding equity for their hires. This simple approach can help to demystify some equity questions. Remember that equity considerations are grounded in the startup or early stage business's valuation and the number of outstanding shares. Since the ownership percentage is determined by the number of shares granted divided by the shares outstanding, keep a careful eye out for dilution, which is the result of a decrease in the value of equity shares though the process of issuing new equity. In the event that a startup or early stage business raises additional funding, the shares outstanding could also increase, reducing ownership.

There are a number of ways to approach equity, including phantom stock, restricted shares, nonqualified options, incentive stock options, and stock appreciation rights (SARs). Not every employee can afford to work without cash compensation, so, with the help of a tax attorney, the founders might consider a balanced solution to meet the needs of the company and potential employees. One possible approach is to determine the number of employees that will receive one to three percent equity. Allow those employees to trade cash for stock during their first three years. The employee will forgo a fixed number of shares for every X amount of cash he or she received over a base figure. A savvy new hire will be thinking about what the shares will be worth in two to 10 years. An experienced advisor can also inform an appropriate vesting schedule, or the amount of equity the employee is entitled to over time. No matter which approach is selected, equity shares should be carefully considered. It is a great option that can help attract, motivate, and retain excellent talent, and should also make sense for your business. Consider building a formula to determine equity based on experience coupled with a salary that you should revisit yearly to adjust for market changes. As you have read in the earlier business case, this approach is best for upper-level management roles in your company.

Equity Legal Thresholds

Private companies are now able to give greater amounts of equity-based compensation to employees, directors, and some consultants without having to share private financials with them. Keep in mind that private companies that have more than 2,000 shareholders are required to register with the SEC as a public company and must provide complete financial transparency.

Benchmark Salary and Equity Data

Large and small organizations have gained tremendous benefit from benchmarking compensation and benefits data. Startups or early stage businesses also need to capitalize on this kind of information. There are a few resources with cash and equity compensation information available that can be used for benchmarking. AngelList, previously mentioned in chapter one, is a great place to start because it provides startup or early stage business salary and equity guidance by role, location, and skills. Venture capital firms also have salary and equity data. They can be goldmines of information if you have already established a relationship. Finally, if you've participated in an accelerator startup program, the advisors, mentors, and staff in these programs are also invaluable resources for compensation data.

At the end of the day, equity-based approaches to compensation are a long-term benefit, and should be offered to folks who you see adding a lot of value to your business. You want them to stick around and contribute to the growth and development of the company. Offering equity is one way of building and promoting loyalty and can be part of a retention strategy.

SHRM Knowledge Domain(s): People
Functional Areas: Total Rewards

PAY EQUITY—OR RATHER, EQUALITY

Pay equity is about having a consistently fair approach to compensating different types of people working for you. Once you're clear on what you can afford to pay, and what you're willing to offer, it's important to also approach compensation with equity. We will discuss risk management in detail in chapter four, but for now we'll highlight a few other laws around pay discrimination. This kind of discrimination can happen based on demographic differentiators like race, age, and gender, among other things. Equal pay has been a headline grabbing issue for decades. Review Table 2.3 for a high-level summary of the relevant laws that ban discrimination in pay.

Understanding and integrating a solid legal scaffold into your company's compensation philosophy is a great way to set your business up for success. As mentioned in chapter one, your organization should seek the support and guidance of an experienced attorney (you can find one from the local bar association) to ensure appropriate compliance in the development of your policies. Also keep in mind that many states have their own equal pay law, which should be included in the compensation strategy. Be especially aware of states that ban employers from asking about salary history, including California, Connecticut, Delaware, Massachusetts, Oregon, and Vermont. For companies with at least five employees, you have the option of performing an internal audit on recent pay decisions. This should be a statistics-based audit. Although most larger businesses could do this in-house, smaller companies might need to hire a consultant for support. The audit should review data on starting pay, recent merit-based pay increases, and recent promotion-based pay increases. Some of the data points will include:

- Unique employee identification number
- Education level at the time of hire
- Gender
- Race/ethnicity
- Salary
- Performance rating

SHRM Knowledge Domain(s): People
Functional Areas: Total Rewards

Internal audits can reveal opportunities for changes to policies and approaches to decision making; however, when it comes to taking actions like increasing salaries, exercise caution. Your team will want to lean on the statistical facts and the support of expert consultants to help identify the right group of employees and the changes needed for corrective action. If your business receives a discrimination charge from the Equal Employment Opportunity Commission (EEOC), take steps to respond to the charges thoughtfully and as soon as possible with the support of legal counsel and your Human Resources team.

Table 2.3. U.S. Laws on Pay Discrimination

U.S. Law	Summary and Description	Caution
Equal Pay Act of 1963 (EPA)	This law prohibits companies from paying women less than men who do the same work at the same location.	Base and justify pay differences by seniority, merit, or incentive systems.
Title VII of the Civil Rights Act of 1964	Bans discrimination of protected groups (race, color, religion, national origin and gender) in all areas of employment, including pay.	Ensure protected groups are not limited to lower paying roles.
Age Discrimination in Employment Act of 1967 (ADEA)	Makes it illegal to make employment related decisions—including compensation—based on age. However, it also allows companies to favor older workers based on age even when doing so adversely affects younger workers.[2]	Base and justify offers, raises, and bonuses on performance or incentive systems.
Americans with Disabilities Act of 1990 (ADA)	The subminimum-wage law for employees with disabilities allows employers to pay less than the minimum wage, although this is being challenged by disability advocates.	Ensure pay to all employees, including protected groups, meets or exceeds the federal requirements.
Lilly Ledbetter Fair Pay Act of 2009	An individual subjected to compensation discrimination under Title VII of the Civil Rights Act of 1964, the Age Discrimination in Employment Act of 1967, or the Americans with Disabilities Act of 1990 may file a charge within 180 (or 300) days of a discriminatory pay-setting decision.[3]	Audit and evaluate company compensation and promotion practices for alignment to federal regulations, internal equity, and external competitiveness. Take corrective action if necessary.

SHRM Knowledge Domain(s): People
Functional Areas: Total Rewards

RESOURCES, TEMPLATES, AND TOOLS FOR COMPENSATION AND BENEFITS
(Items in italics can be found in the appendix.)

Compensation and Employee Benefits
Total Compensation Statement

Sample Policies
Merit Increase Policy and Procedure
Performance and Salary Review Policy

ADDITIONAL TOOLS

Table 2.4. Basic Compensation Philosophy Statement Checklist
Use the following checklist to write a basic compensation philosophy.

Element	General Content
Rationale	Reason for having a compensation program
Key Connections	How the program will support the business objectives
Salary Benchmarks	How to compensate for performance (e.g. aspects of incentive pay)
Exceptional Candidates or Performance	This is where you mention any special requirements or experience for the project
Employee Knowledge	The levels to which employees will be educated on the compensation philosophy
	The levels of transparency with compensation
When to Revisit	The frequency of compensation reviews

REFERENCES

Internal Revenue Service. "Employer Shared Responsibility Provisions." Accessed March 28, 2019. https://www.irs.gov/affordable-care-act/employers/employer-shared-responsibility-provisions.

Miller, Stephen. "SEC Eases Small-Business Disclosures for Stock-Based Compensation." Society for Human Resource Management. July 26, 2018. https://www.shrm.org/resourcesandtools/hr-topics/

compensation/pages/sec-final-rule-equity-compensation-disclosures.aspx.

Society for Human Resource Management. "How to Establish Salary Ranges." Accessed May 23, 2018. https://www.shrm.org/ resourcesandtools/tools-and-samples/how-to-guides/pages/ howtoestablishsalaryranges.aspx.

U.S. Equal Employment Opportunity Commission. "Facts About Age Discrimination." Accessed March 28, 2019. https://www.eeoc.gov/ eeoc/publications/age.cfm.

U.S. Equal Employment Opportunity Commission. "Notice Concerning the Lilly Ledbetter Fair Pay Act of 2009." Accessed March 28, 2019. https://www.eeoc.gov/laws/statutes/epa_ ledbetter.cfm.

ENDNOTES

1. "Employer Shared Responsibility Provisions," Internal Revenue Service, accessed March 28, 2019, https://www.irs.gov/affordable-care-act/employers/employer-shared-responsibility-provisions.
2. "Facts About Age Discrimination," U.S. Equal Employment Opportunity Commission, accessed March 28, 2019, https://www.eeoc.gov/eeoc/publications/age.cfm.
3. "Notice Concerning the Lilly Ledbetter Fair Pay Act of 2009," U.S. Equal Employment Opportunity Commission, accessed March 28, 2019, https://www.eeoc.gov/laws/statutes/epa_ledbetter.cfm.

ADDITIONAL INSIGHT ON BENEFITS

Choosing and Building Benefits Coverage: A Broker's Insight

Karen Southers, an insurance broker, has helped startup, early stage, and small business clients with as few as two employees find and purchase the right level of benefits related insurance policies for their company. Unlike the larger national brokers, her firm will enroll anyone to start a group health plan, as long as they meet the criteria set in place by the various insurance carriers. The basic requirements to write a group health policy are that the company provide their tax reports from the prior year, for sole-proprietor group health plans, or provide a copy of their business license, incorporation papers, or IRS Form SS-4. Depending on the carrier, the underwriting process for disability policies can be a bit more rigid. In fact, there are certain "high-risk" areas that may only be approved by ancillary carriers that would do the underwriting for a disability policy, such as steelworkers or truck drivers. Other underwriters would automatically decline the coverage. However, when it comes to health policies, Southers' company can write health policies for anyone. There are no preexisting condition clauses that would prevent the development of a health policy for anyone.

How the Affordable Care Act Impacted Small Businesses and Brokers

When the Affordable Care Act started in January of 2014, Southers' company had a lot of smaller clients (clients with a few employees) that had never had health insurance in place before and were reaching out with an interest in getting a group health plan. Before this change in legislation, it was more common to see the business owner with an individual policy, that covered his/her spouse, but their business didn't provide any coverage for employees, even though it was something that employees were practically demanding.

The Affordable Care Act's individual mandate opened up new opportunities for small businesses that never had health coverage in 20 years of operation, and kept it even after the individual mandate was dropped in 2019. Business owners worry about if continuing the coverage makes sense, so they'll quote all their employees and ask a broker "What would it look like if we went individual?" It could be anywhere from 10–15 employees, but Southers' company will quote all of them with individual policies to help the business owners make an informed choice, because it can get pretty expensive. Although a business doesn't have to pay anything toward dependents, some groups are required to pay at least 50 percent of the cost of employee-only coverage.

A Case of High-Deductibles and Reimbursement.

Karen had a group client with about 15 employees. Their policy had a $6,000 deductible for individuals and $12,000 deductible for families. However, this company reimbursed 100% of deductible expenses. Since the out-of-pocket maximum on that plan was also $6,000 for individuals and $12,000 for families, once an employee met that amount, the insurance kicked in and payed 100 percent of the remaining prescription and medical expenses that are in-network for the rest of the plan year. An employee in this group had a spouse that delivered a baby by C-section. Having a C-section delivery is much more expensive than a natural birth and requires a longer recovery time. This employee's spouse stayed in the hospital for an extended period of time and, as a result, ended up meeting their family's $12,000 deductible that year. The health reimbursement arrangement then paid all of those expenses. Eventually, that employee found another job about six months after the birth of the baby, but came back to his previous employer. He had a conversation with Karen about what brought him back. He said, "I never realized how good my insurance was until I left." She echoed that he did have very good insurance. His new employers only paid 75% of employee-only costs and didn't pay anything toward dependents. Coming back was a no brainer.

Brokers as Your Intermediary

Many small group clients don't have an official HR department or a manager, so oftentimes, the owner or the spouse of the owner tries to fill the shoes of the HR department. A broker can step in and take on that responsibility, get information on multiple insurance carriers plan comparisons very quickly, and can provide more of a customer service role as well. Karen has been a consistent point of contact for many employees who may have questions about coverage.

Lessons Learned

- Depending on the broker, small businesses can get covered for a few as two employees
- Although the Affordable Care Act individual mandate was removed in 2019, individual coverage can still be purchased by businesses
- The quality of the health insurance can have a tremendous impact on retention
- Brokers can serve as an intermediary by taking on the role of an HR department

CHAPTER 3

The "Soft" Side

HOW TO GIVE FEEDBACK AND SET GOALS
FOR A HIGH-PERFORMANCE TEAM

William J. Rothwell

QUICK-START GUIDE TO THE "SOFT" SIDE

Chapter Three in a Nutshell

Companies of every size have to figure out the best ways to evaluate an employee's job performance, build and sustain employee engagement, reduce avoidable turnover, and ensure accountability.

To do so, you will need to:

- Establish a consistent process to manage employee performance
- Address employee engagement
- Ensure employee retention
- Hold people accountable for their work

This chapter focuses on these areas and other related topics.

Promotions Can Be Problematic: Performance
Management Business Case and Lessons Learned

A training company in the Midwest hired a director that came highly recommended. Things were going well in the beginning, but it wasn't long before her performance started to dwindle. Despite that, she was promoted from working solo to managing a team. She was soon known for her micromanagement and began to have several issues with her team members. Things got to the point where a male team member filed a grievance against her for sexual harassment. After an internal investigation, it was confirmed that her behavior was inappropriate, but it was not to the point where it was sexual harassment. As the months went by, her performance continued to be poor. Her direct manager gave her some verbal feedback and sent a few emails, but didn't go so far as to formally document the performance issues and nothing had gone through HR. By the time the company got to the end of year evaluations to give raises, she got an increase. It turned out it wasn't a merit or performance-based increase, but a cost of living increase that everyone received, even though she'd had these performance issues.

SHRM Knowledge Domain(s): People
Functional Areas: Employee Engagement

Firing Failure

A few months into the new year, the employee's manager had enough and he decided to fire her with an offer of four weeks of severance and a requirement that she sign a waiver of release from any further legal action. She had 14 days to sign the waiver, and at that point in time the manager finally brought in HR. The employee did not sign the waiver, and she proceeded to sue the company for wrongful termination.

The process was handled through mediation, and the only documentation that the company had were the emails her manager sent. The fired employee argued that she was wrongfully terminated, and emphasized her increase in salary. The company ended up paying a settlement that was basically the same four weeks she was offered initially, minus her legal fees.

Lessons Learned

- Promoting someone that has performance issues is never a good idea.
- Sending emails isn't enough to document poor performance. Proper documentation includes the specific issues and a performance plan or feedback that you've shared.
- Not involving your HR team early on when performance concerns come up can cost the company time, effort, and money.
- Promoting an employee without understanding if he or she has the right skills for the role sets up the employee—and the company—for failure.
- Using *progressive discipline* is important. You should go from a verbal discussion to written warnings, and then an action plan of what you'd like to see happen in a specific timeframe.

Every business, no matter the size, needs to have clear and solid ways to evaluate job performance. There's no doubt that this can be intimidating. You might be asking questions like, "How do I actually rate job performance? What's the best way to hold workers accountable? What can I do to get and keep my team engaged? What do I do when discipline is necessary? How can I keep talented people from leaving?" This chapter addresses these questions.

SHRM Knowledge Domain(s): People
Functional Areas: Employee Engagement

EVALUATING STAFF PERFORMANCE AND IMPACT

We define *performance management* as a continuing process of communication between workers and their immediate supervisors. The goal is to help plan, monitor, evaluate, and reward behavior and outcomes. A *performance management system* contains the policies and procedures made to guide performance management in an organization.

In chapter one, we talked about how a job description helps communicate with people outside of the company what talent is needed, and also helps an employee understand the work they need to do. A *performance review,* on the other hand, will let an employee evaluate work performance over a period of time and learn what kind of development is needed to prepare for the future. Performance management can be thought of in a cycle and has at least four steps:

- **Align** your company's strategic goals and an individual employee's work requirements
- **Plan** work targets in a way that is measurable
- **Monitor** how the work requirements are achieved over a specific timeframe
- **Evaluate** how well work targets are achieved during that same timeframe

Those are the basics, but you can add additional steps to the cycle like planning, monitoring, and evaluating how well a workers' job performance aligns with organizational values and ethics.

Making Performance Management Work

Performance management can vary depending on:

- Who is the focus of the performance management
- What performance is targeted for management
- The duration of performance to be managed
- Where the performance management system is targeted

- Why performance management is happening and what results are expected
- How the performance management is carried out

Who is the focus of the performance management means that performance management systems might be directed to different targeted groups in the organization. Things tend to get less rigid the higher up the food chain. Generally, the higher the position on the organization chart, the less likely that role is subject to performance management in spite of the fact that higher-level positions have the most alignment between their job duties and the company's strategic goals.

What performance is targeted for management means the specific good and bad results or behaviors of an employee that your company will focus on for evaluation. *Behaviors* are observable actions; *results* are measurable outputs associated with the employees' behaviors.

The duration of performance to be managed refers to time. It's common for most companies to review a workers' job performance annually. But, this is not a requirement. In fact, for some senior-level jobs—like a CEO or CFO—the amount of time it takes to see the impact of results may take much longer than one year to measure, and can be as long as four years. The fancy term for this is the *timespan of discretion*. For employees at lower levels on the organization chart, the timespan of discretion would be much less.

Where the performance management system is targeted refers to the location scope of the performance review. For example, will the review focus on a specific area, such as one plant, or a specific geographic region? If your business is international, will it focus on one country? Larger companies may find it worthwhile to build different performance management systems to comply with local employment laws.

Why performance management is happening and what results are expected refers to the reasons why the performance management program was made. You'll have to figure out if the goal is to control behavior, individual development, or a combination of both. Here are some possible focused goals of a performance management program:

- Planning for future job performance by setting measurable targets
- Finding ways to monitor job performance during the performance review period
- Evaluating results against targets
- Pinpointing barriers to job performance that prevent employees from achieving results
- Identifying training needs
- Justifying salary changes
- Making the case for corrective action
- Identifying individuals for promotion
- Providing specific feedback for improvement or for development through coaching, counseling, or mentoring
- Aligning individual job performance with organizational strategic goals, divisional or departmental goals, and/or team goals

How the performance management is carried out is addressed by creating a written policy statement that describes the purpose of the performance management program and the goals that will be achieved from it. The policy statement would describe:

- Who should conduct performance management reviews
- What should be the focus of those reviews
- When planning, monitoring, and reviewing will be carried out each year
- Where the review will take place
- How performance reviews will be conducted
- What decisions will be made during the performance reviews
- When and how the performance reviews will be securely stored

Your company can do more than one kind of performance review. For example, the *annual review* would focus on an employee's yearly job performance. *Project reviews* would be done at the end of a project by a team leader or by team members evaluating each other. There are also *introductory reviews* that examine how well workers perform during the initial months on the job (introductory period) or after a promotion. Finally, *training reviews* can occur periodically (weekly) during a training period for a specific job.

Choosing What to Review

Organizational leaders have many options from which to choose regarding what is reviewed. Typical methods include:

- 360-degree assessment
- Self-evaluation
- Manager evaluation
- Behavioral list
- Rating scales

A *360-degree assessment* begins with a self-evaluation that will then be compared with averaged scores that came from feedback from an employee's managers, leaders, peers, and subordinates. The *self-evaluation* is completed by individuals on themselves; a *manager evaluation* is completed by managers on their team members. *Behavioral lists* invite people to rate and assess an employee against a list of behaviors. *Rating scales* may vary in what they rate, but common rating scales are often presented along a continuum:

0 = Not applicable

1 = Falls far below expectations

2 = Falls below expectations

3 = Meets expectations

4 = Exceeds expectations

5 = Far exceeds expectations.

No performance management system is perfect. But the system's value depends not so much on the "form" (what is rated) as on the "process" (how the performance management system is implemented). While there is more than one way to organize a performance appraisal meeting, the most common approach is the so-called "sandwich structure." In the sandwich structure, the person giving the evaluation begins the performance review meeting with small talk. That is the top of the sandwich. Then the rater turns to the "meat"—commentary about what is good and what needs improvement about the workers' job performance. While that section can include some level of constructive criticism, it's important to pair any criticism with specific advice about what needs to change, what results to achieve, or other coaching information to ensure that the employee is clear on what's expected and how to get there. The final section of the performance appraisal meeting is the bottom of the sandwich and consists of what will happen next. It may indicate how the worker will receive written comments or may provide an opportunity for the employee to comment and then sign a form for record keeping.

Before you use the "sandwich structure" or set up a meeting, it's important to be well prepared and plan, plan, plan. Start by reviewing the employees' performance records and any written documentation about job performance that has been noted over the course of the review period. Don't ignore performance issues, and make sure they are documented and discussed. Remember that positive feedback can do a ton for morale, so be sure to highlight any special achievements the employee received.

> *You may have heard of the sandwich method, but don't misunderstand it. There are other methods to giving feedback or for use in performance reviews, such as the start, stop, and continue method. With this method, you share exactly what you need the employee to start doing, stop doing, and continue doing.*

BUILDING AND SUSTAINING EMPLOYEE ENGAGEMENT

Every leader has an obligation to build and sustain a culture and climate that inspires employee engagement. As noted in chapter one, *culture* is basically "how we do things around here." It is an unspoken code that guides behavior. *Climate*, on the other hand, is best understood as "how people feel around here right now." Culture is like an individual's personality, and climate can be compared to an individual's mood. *Employee engagement* refers to how much passionate commitment people feel about the organizational context. More than morale, engagement implies alignment between the individual's self-identity and organizational identity.[1]

Generally speaking, engagement is a problem for a number of companies. Employees are less engaged than their leaders wish they were. However, things are looking up, and the results of a 2018 Gallup study on engagement showed that the U.S. economy improved engagement of U.S. workers; 34 percent of U.S. workers are engaged and only 14 percent of U.S. workers are actively disengaged.[2] Engaged workers have lower turnover, lower accident rates, higher productivity, higher profitability, higher customer satisfaction scores, and much more (Harter, 2018). But how do leaders build and sustain an engaged work culture? While the question is simple, the answer is not. It requires action in every area where an organization "touches" its people: during recruiting, selecting, onboarding, training, evaluating, rewarding, managing, and letting people go. Every aspect of the company must be organized in a way to encourage engagement and discourage disengagement.

GETTING EMPLOYEES TO STAY

When the leaders in a company invest in developing and engaging workers, they want them to stay with the organization. *Turnover* refers to the percentage of workers who leave during a specific period of time. Although turnover is sometimes categorized as avoidable or unavoidable, normally it's assumed that leaders are referring to avoidable turnover. It is calculated by dividing the number of resignations in the organization over the total headcount of workers in a given timespan and then multiplying by 100. The sum of that calculation is the *avoidable turnover*.

Improving Retention

So, how can organizations improve employee retention? (1) Measure employee engagement and take proactive steps to improve it, and (2) improve the way exit interviews are done. Remember, reducing turnover and improving engagement requires action in every area in which an organization "touches" its people: during recruiting, selecting, onboarding, training, evaluating, rewarding, managing, and letting people go. When screening applicants, look for patterns like multiple jobs in a short period of time. When onboarding workers, pay as much attention to how they got along with others and the culture overall. People are more likely to leave an organization when they have few social relationships. One way to help employees make connections is to create a peer mentoring program where workers are connected to peer mentors whose "welcome wagon" job is to help them acclimate.

Although a lot of organizations have good recruitment and training systems, fewer actually devote the same amount of time and attention to retention. Most of the time, someone with HR responsibilities conducts an exit interview with a worker leaving the company on the last day, week, or month on the job. Unfortunately, a *social desirability bias* can occur, which is when people tell someone that is asking them questions what they think they want them to say. People leaving a company worry about how the things they say will be used and how that information might affect their references or possibility of getting rehired. As a result, people give socially desirable answers to questions in exit interviews.

To improve exit interviews, managers with HR responsibility shouldn't do the exit interview on an employees' last day, week, or month of employment. Instead, send a survey to them about three weeks after their last day on the job. If your business can create a secure link, go for it. If not, a paper form with a place to drop it off or mail it back would also work well.

Talking with the employee's former manager can also provide useful information, as they might have learned the reasons why the employee decided to leave. This is helpful because some employees might not share the same information with an HR professional that they would with their peers or manager. Retention also requires attention to details. How well are new hires fitting in? How well are their problems addressed soon after they come up? Do new hires feel comfortable to ask questions, approach their immediate supervisors, and talk to their coworkers? If no, then turnover is likely to be high.

SHRM Knowledge Domain(s): People
Functional Areas: Employee Engagement

DISCIPLINE AND DOCUMENTATION

Few managers enjoy *discipline*—otherwise known as *corrective action*. However, it is a common process used to bring employee behaviors into alignment with a company's work rules and requirements. Generally, corrective action issues fall into two categories: (1) behavioral and (2) performance-related.

Behavioral problems are common—and are the bane of nearly every manager's existence! Examples of behavioral problems include:

- Lateness (tardiness)
- Abuse of sick time (absenteeism)
- Issues associated with attire
- Issues associated with customer service

Examples of performance problems are associated with employees who, despite having received appropriate training and appropriate communication about expected job performance, consistently fail to get expected work results.

It's up to the leadership in your company to establish disciplinary or corrective action policies and procedures and then require that those policies are consistently applied by managers across the organization. Two kinds of disciplinary philosophies are popular in organizations today. One is called positive discipline; the other, progressive discipline.

Positive discipline involves giving workers participation in the decision-making process.

It is typically carried out in a three-step process when applied to organizational settings and used to encourage alignment with behavioral and job performance expectations. The first step is to communicate behavioral and performance expectations clearly. After all, employees cannot achieve targets that require guessing games to figure out. The second step is to rely on coaching to question workers on how their behavior or performance might impact others. In other words, workers are shown how their behavior or performance helps to achieve organizational goals and what happens to others (and to the organization) when

SHRM Knowledge Domain(s): People
Functional Areas: Employee Engagement

the workers depart from requirements. The goal is to show employees why they must behave and perform in certain ways and how failure to do so may negatively affect other people or the organization. The third and final step of positive discipline is to enlist the help of workers to find ways to bring their behaviors or performance into alignment with organizational requirements. Positive discipline takes its name from an emphasis on providing positive reinforcement to recognize behavior and performance that is aligned with organizational requirements. Instead of looking for workers who are failing to meet requirements and then devoting time to punishing them, positive discipline emphasizes the value of finding workers who are acting in ways that are good or excellent and then highlighting what they do or what they achieve to others.

Progressive discipline is what most startups and small business owners would have time for and has long been the standard approach to corrective action. It does not emphasize punishment; instead, the focus is on identifying and solving problems with work behaviors or job performance. Repeated violations of problematic behaviors or job performance results trigger steps in the progressive disciplinary process. The goal is to give workers coaching to solve their problems and ample time to do so.

The manager should give a worker a verbal warning with the first indication of a problematic behavior or upon the first occasion that supervisors notice a job performance problem. With this warning, a supervisor simply tells the worker that he or she is not behaving or performing as expected. If the problem does not happen again, that is the last step in the progressive discipline process.

But, if the problem recurs, supervisors move on to a written warning. In a written warning, supervisors typically spell out:

- What the employee is doing (describes the behavior or job performance problem)
- What the employee should do (describes the relevant organizational work rule or performance standard)
- What is the measurable gap between what the employee is doing and what the employee should be doing

- Why the gap is important (What are the consequences or impact of the gap?)
- How to close the gap (provide coaching on ways to close the gap)
- How much time will be allowed between the write-up and the next occurrence
- What will happen upon the next occurrence

It should be mentioned that many disciplinary issues can go unresolved for several reasons. One reason is that managers may be reluctant to ask for help with the disciplinary problems they face with their workers for fear that their own supervisors will think that they are not capable of handling tough "people" problems. A second reason that managers suffer with problematic behavior is that they worry that their own superiors will not support them in the disciplinary action they wish to take. It is simply easier in many cases to suffer the problems with workers than deal with the politics of the organization. However, it's better for managers to think about how to overcome these problems.

MOVING TO TERMINATION

Letting people go can be tough. Employees typically have their employment terminated as the final step in the disciplinary or corrective action process. Since it is time-consuming and costly to hire, onboard, and train workers, managers are typically reluctant to fire people. Nevertheless, there are times when it is warranted. Termination is warranted in two cases: workers, after receiving multiple chances to correct problematic behaviors or performance, fail to change. The second case is when workers violate a work rule and moving to termination is activated without warning. Only a few such cases are typically explicitly outlined in organization's HR policies and procedures:

- Violence in the workplace
- Threats of violence
- Sexual harassment
- Stealing

- Watching pornography in the workplace
- Falsifying books or records
- Insubordination
- Failing drug or alcohol tests
- Creating a safety hazard

There can be other violations, but those should be stipulated in the organization's employee handbook. However, keep in mind that there are exceptions under U.S. law to the so-called *employment-at-will principle* (more in chapter four) in which workers may be fired for good, bad, or no causes. Workers should not be fired, or threatened with firing, if:

- Company policy is not followed (for example, workers are told they will only be fired under certain conditions)
- The worker is behaving in ways aligned with a public policy (for instance, workers cannot be fired for filing for workers compensation)
- The worker is whistleblowing (that is, blowing the whistle on employer wrongdoing)
- The worker does not comply with a demand for sexual favors
- The worker is protected by law (such as being pregnant, over the age of 40, and so forth)
- The worker is terminated against the stipulations of a union's collective bargaining agreement

Eleven states in the United States require employers to act in accordance with a covenant of Good Faith and Fair Dealing. Those states include Alabama, Alaska, Arizona, California, Delaware, Idaho, Massachusetts, Nevada, Montana, Utah, and Wyoming. As you read in the performance management business case at the beginning of this chapter, workers in the Unites States can file a lawsuit if they think they have been unjustly treated in their termination.

USING CONSULTANTS TO BUILD HR POLICIES AND SYSTEMS

Benefits Business Case and Lessons Learned

Maria Rodriguez is the chief executive officer of a fast-growth chain of grocery stores in the inner cities of Michigan. The first store grew from her experiences in childhood when she observed her mother's difficulties looking for groceries. To solve the problem, Maria gave such tight security to a local inner-city store that people called it "The Fort." Others joked that the security in the store was tighter than that of a police station. But the concept worked, and the store grew into a chain.

Growing Pains

As her chain grew, it soon became apparent that the human resources system was far from up-to-date. Workers were hired without any regard to their backgrounds, and their pay was negotiated without any organized paygrades in place. It was bewildering to everyone when workers compared paychecks and people doing the same work were paid vastly different rates.

Maria hired a consultant to help her launch an HR system. She wanted to ensure that one or more systems were in place to hold workers accountable for doing their jobs, so she asked the consultants to give her proposals on launching a performance management system, an employee engagement program, and a corrective action/employee disciplinary system.

The consultants began their work by writing an employee handbook to cover all HR policies and practices for the company. Then, they formed committees of managers and employees from the stores to prepare draft proposals for supervisor and worker performance management systems, an employee engagement program, and a corrective action/employee disciplinary system. The consultants ensured that managers and employees understood the system and gave senior managers a chance to make changes in these systems. The consultants also gave the company outlines to guide training programs for performance management, employee engagement, and corrective action.

Lessons Learned

For this company, hiring a consulting team helped the business do the following:

- Create several important HR resources in a short timeframe.

- Pull together team members across the organization to help shape the resources that they have to use.

- Give employees an opportunity to ask questions about the new process, which is important when introducing new systems. This will allow you to make any additional updates or changes before a formal roll out.

(continued)

SHRM Knowledge Domain(s): People
Functional Areas: Employee Engagement

Lessons Learned

For this company, hiring a consulting team helped the business do the following:

- Create several important HR resources in a short timeframe.

- Pull together team members across the organization to help shape the resources that they have to use.

- Give employees an opportunity to ask questions about the new process, which is important when introducing new systems. This will allow you to make any additional updates or changes before a formal roll out.

RESOURCES, TEMPLATES, AND TOOLS FOR MANAGING THE "SOFT" SIDE

(Items in italics can be found in the appendix.)

Performance Management Systems
Completed Performance Appraisal Form
Performance Appraisal Form
Performance Appraisal Form (including supervisory skills)
Performance Review Meeting Checklist

Employee Engagement Programs
Mark Feffer, "Fixing Poor Engagement Starts with Understanding Its Cause," https://www.shrm.org/resourcesandtools/hr-topics/employee-relations/pages/how-to-fix-poor-employee-engagement.aspx

Disciplinary Policies, Procedures and Programs
Performance Improvement Plan 1
Performance Improvement Plan 2
Progressive Discipline Policy

Termination Procedures
Separation of Employment Policy—Procedures for Voluntary and Involuntary Terminations

REFERENCES

Harter, Jim. "Employee Engagement on the Rise in the U.S." Accessed June 2, 2019. https://news.gallup.com/poll/241649/employee-engagement-rise.aspx.

Rothwell, William, J. *Creating Engaged Employees: It's Worth the Investment.* Alexandria: ASTD Press, 2014.

ENDNOTES

1. William J. Rothwell, *Creating Engaged Employees: It's Worth the Investment* (Alexandria: ASTD Press, 2014).
2. Jim Harter, "Employee Engagement on the Rise in the U.S.," accessed June 2, 2019, https://news.gallup.com/poll/241649/employee-engagement-rise.aspx.

SHRM Knowledge Domain(s): People
Functional Areas: Employee Engagement

PART II

LEGAL AND WORKFORCE PLANNING FOR GROWTH STAGE BUSINESSES

Legal

ALL THE STUFF YOU SHOULD KNOW BUT PROBABLY DON'T

Marie Carasco

QUICK-START GUIDE TO LEGAL

Chapter Four in a Nutshell

It's in the best interest of your organization to develop a solid understanding of U.S. employment law to manage risk in the people-side of operations.

To do so, you will need to:

- Understand how to apply the Family and Medical Leave Act (FMLA) and the Fair Labor Standards Act (FLSA)
- Stay in compliance with the Americans with Disabilities Act (ADA)
- Carefully navigate employment-at-will and know what is allowed to avoid unlawful or discriminatory practices
- Create a risk management plan to prepare for interruptions to work-flow and productivity
- Acquire workers' compensation insurance based on your states' laws
- Know your rights as an employer when it comes to union development employers

This chapter focuses on these areas and other related topics.

What You Don't Know Will Hurt You: Union Interactions
Business Case and Lessons Learned

James runs a growing manufacturing company in the Southwest. When he started out, he was focused on getting the business going and didn't pay a lot of attention to anything besides getting the job done. He needed hard working people who didn't care too much about the kind of benefits that larger companies would give, because the business couldn't afford it. In spite of that, the pay was reasonable for the area. It wasn't long before some leaders on the manufacturing floor convinced the employees that they weren't being heard. Until that point, James was the kind of person who listened to what people had to say, but his role changed and he wasn't as visible on the floor anymore. There was no HR department, and no one had stepped up to fill that gap. In hindsight, that should have been given more attention. There should have been someone on the startup team who had either the temperament or skill sets of an HR manager, who could also do the other work that needed to be done. There wasn't a transition plan to take on the HR things that James did, and the employees had no one to go to.

Organizing Activities Sometimes Comes from a New Hire

The employees found someone to listen, and it wasn't long before one of the new hires started encouraging the idea of unionizing. Meetings started happening in an open bar setting, with promises of all kinds of lofty benefits: double pay, pension plans, Cadillac healthcare plans. They promised them if they would elect a union, they could get literally everything that they wanted.

The election process started with the National Labor Relations Board (NLRB), but James had no idea what was happening. He would soon find out that 50 percent of the employees needed to sign voting cards to move forward in a union election process. Things progressed pretty quickly. The NLRB faxed a document that said that the company was now under a union election process, but it went to the wrong fax number so no one in leadership knew. Things got even trickier when there were several attempts to invalidate the election so that the election would be eliminated and the company would get automatically unionized.

James got a call from the union rep, who didn't mention anything about the election, but simply said he'd been contacted by people at the company. The union rep asked James if he would like to sit down with him to discuss the issues that they're having, and James agreed to a meeting. However, James got a call from someone at the Labor Relations Institute (LRI) shortly afterwards that would change everything.

The Tables Turn

The LRI told James that his business had been petitioned to be unionized and that they informed about it. They told James everything that would happen, including the invitation from the union rep, and advised him not to attend that meeting because the rep would ask James if he wanted to know who was bringing the concerns up. The LRI let James know that if he were to physically look at the cards with the names of the employees on them, he would invalidate the election because it would no longer be a secret ballot. James learned that he had to be careful in the ways he responded because the process was so delicate, and the LRI explained what not to do with the acronym TIPS. No threats, interrogation, promises, or surveillance.

Fast forward to a 40-day election process. James created a 4 to 5-week plan that was designed to help employees make their own conclusions. One of the most powerful things he did was opening up the company finances, showing where every penny went and the reality of the financial situation. They were barely getting by. James also shared true stories of what happened in other companies that unionized.

Things Got Contentious

A lawsuit was filed after James fired someone on the day the company should have received the union election paperwork, but it had nothing to do with the union process. The case was thrown out because the company had detailed HR documentation on the former employee's poor performance.

On election day, there were protestors who told employees the company hated them and made it very difficult and intimidating to physically get to the voting booth. But at the end of the day, James and his team won the election and the company didn't unionize. They were able to turn the corner financially and now have some of the best wages and benefits in the area. They also spend a lot of time on employee engagement, using a survey called AMP every quarter to see how people are feeling, evaluate their stress levels, and make sure that employees are being listened to. In the end, the process helped build a better company.

Lessons Learned

- Never leave the HR related work unattended. If you're not going to have somebody who's directly titled as the HR manager, someone on the team who enjoys talking to people and can navigate complex emotional situations should wear that hat.

SHRM Knowledge Domain(s): Workplace; Organization; Strategy
Functional Areas: U.S. Employment Law and Regulations, Risk Mngt., Business and HR Strategy, Employee Relations

- Take time to understand the needs and interests of your employees and what makes unionizing attractive.
- Leverage the right legal advice to understand the process and create a planned response.
- Create opportunities for employees to be heard.
- Document performance issues properly in the event of a wrongful termination lawsuit.

PART ONE: LEGAL HEAVY HITTERS AND FUNDAMENTALS IN U.S. EMPLOYMENT LAW

No company wants an unnecessary legal battle. In fact, it might be in the best interest of your organization to develop a solid understanding of legal heavy hitters in U.S. employment law to help manage risk in the people-side of operations. Although there are a lot of federal statues out there, this chapter will cover the foundational regulations for a new and growing company.

Family and Medical Leave Act (FMLA)

Sometimes an employee or their loved ones can be too ill to work. If your company has 50 or more employees that worked for at least 20 weeks in this current or prior year, these employees are eligible by law to receive the benefits of the Family and Medical Leave Act (FMLA). The U.S. Department of Labor outlines that eligible employees would be able to:

- Take up to 12 work weeks of unpaid time off each year for family and medical reasons
- Retain the same group health insurance benefits
- Return to their current role or an equivalent role after the FMLA has ended

Employees in military families can take additional time of up to 26 weeks to care for an injured or ill military service member. Although FMLA is unpaid leave, your company can "require the employee to use accrued paid vacation leave, paid sick leave, or family leave for some or all of the FMLA leave period."[1] Depending on the medical situation, the employee can take the leave in separate blocks of time and not necessarily all at once. If it is clear that the employee will have a planned medical procedure, all parties should coordinate a schedule in the best way possible to minimize disruptions to business operations. If your company doesn't already have one, "employers should have a well-written policy regarding leaves of absence and require employees to provide updates on their return-to-work status...An employer may but is not required to have a return-to-work certification requirement as part of its FMLA leave policy. Under the policy, employers may require workers to provide certification from their health care provider stating that they are able to resume work. Keep in mind that in some states, such as California, employers can't ask for medical diagnosis information or communicate with the employee's doctor about the employee's medical condition without the employee's consent. Employers should use forms that are compliant with the California Family Rights Act, rather than the FMLA, so they don't ask unauthorized questions under state law.[2] See Exhibit 4.1 for a FMLA compliance checklist.

You might be wondering how to define a serious health condition. The U.S. Department of Labor outlines conditions that qualify for FMLA leave as:

- conditions requiring an overnight stay in a hospital or other medical care facility;
- conditions that incapacitate you or your family member (for example, being unable to work or attend school) for more than three consecutive days and having ongoing medical treatment (either multiple appointments with a health care provider, or a single appointment and follow-up care, such as prescription medication);
- chronic conditions that cause occasional periods when you or your family member are incapacitated and require treatment by a health care provider at least twice a year; and

- pregnancy (including prenatal medical appointments, incapacity due to morning sickness, and medically required bed rest).[3]

See Table 4.4 for a FMLA employee eligibility checklist at the end of the chapter.

To learn more about the FMLA, visit the U.S. Department of Labor website (www.dol.gov/whd). The Wage and Hour Division will navigate you to FLMA general and interpretive guidance, fact sheets, e-tools, posters, forms, and other applicable laws and regulations.

Fair Labor Standards Act (FLSA)

You might have heard people in operations, finance, or human resources teams use the phrases "exempt" and "nonexempt" employees—phrases part of the Fair Labor Standards Act (FLSA). This law was signed in the late 1930s and established many of the regulations that have been long forgotten. It prohibits child labor and it established minimum wages, record-keeping, overtime rates, and a limited work week. The phrases "exempt" and "nonexempt" refer to employee eligibility for overtime based on the classification of work they do, particularly white collar versus blue collar, respectively. Here are some detailed definitions from the Society for Human Resource Management's HR Q&A.[4]

Exempt

An individual who meets specific criteria and is exempt from the overtime provisions of the FLSA due to classification as an executive, professional, administrative or outside sales employee. Certain computer professionals may also be exempt. With some limited exceptions, exempt employees must be paid on a salary basis (see www.dol.gov/whd/overtime/fs17g_salary.pdf).

Nonexempt

An individual who is not exempt from the overtime provisions of the FLSA and is therefore entitled to overtime pay for all hours worked beyond 40 in a workweek (as well as any state overtime provisions). Nonexempt employees may be paid on a salary, hourly, or other basis.

Salaried

An individual who receives the same salary from week to week regardless of total worked hours. Exempt employees must be paid on a salary basis, as discussed above. Nonexempt employees may be paid on a salary basis for a fixed number of hours or under the fluctuating workweek method. Salaried nonexempt employees must still receive overtime in accordance with federal and state laws.

Hourly

An individual who receives an hourly wage for work performed. Generally, such employees, due to the method of payment, are classified as nonexempt and are subject to the overtime provisions of the FLSA. Exempt computer professionals may also be paid on an hourly basis, as could those exempt under the professional exemption, such as teachers, lawyers, and doctors.

The FLSA "prescribes standards for wages and overtime pay, which affect most private and public employment [and] it requires employers to pay covered employees who are not otherwise exempt at least the federal minimum wage and overtime pay of one-and-one-half-times the regular rate of pay. For nonagricultural operations, it restricts the hours that children under age 16 can work and forbids the employment of children under age 18 in certain jobs deemed too dangerous. For agricultural operations, it prohibits the employment of children under age 16 during school hours and in certain jobs deemed too dangerous."[5] See Figure 4.1 for a summary of the types of entities required to comply with the FLSA.

So, what exactly are you as an employer required to do under the FLSA? Well, all employees that work for companies like those described in the general guidance figure are covered by the FLSA.

To learn more about the FLSA, visit the U.S. Department of Labor website (www.dol.gov/whd). Go to the Wage and Hour Division to navigate to the FLSA Compliance Assistance page for fact sheets, references guides,

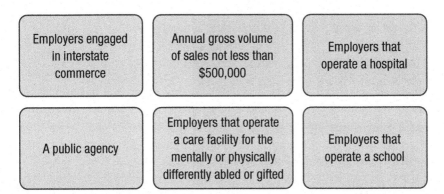

Figure 4.1. Summary of the Types of Entities Required to Comply with the FLSA

employment law guides, information on furloughs and other reductions in pay, break time for nursing mothers, posters, e-tools, and cards on how to file a complaint (available in multiple languages). The Wage and Hour Division produces a digital reference guide to the FLSA. You can also call toll-free at 1-866-487-9243 (1-866-4US-WAGE), TDD: 1-877-889-5627.

Workplace Accommodations and Americans with Disabilities Act (ADA)

Over the course of the life cycle of your business, you will encounter employees who are differently abled, or current team members who experience a life event that will change the ways they can accomplish their work. The federal government refers to people with physical or mental limitations as disabled. The Americans with Disabilities Act of 1990 (ADA) prohibits discrimination against those with disabilities and requires employers to provide reasonable accommodations. If your company is engaged in interstate commerce and has 15 or more employees, ADA applies to you. However, keep in mind that "some states also have antidiscrimination laws in place for all employers, even those with one employee."[6] ADA applies protection to people that meet the definition of a disability in one of three categories (see Figure 4.2).

"For an employee or job applicant to be protected by the ADA, an individual must be 'disabled' in one or more of the above manners, be 'otherwise qualified' for the position, and be able to perform the essential functions of the job, 'with or without accommodation.'"[7] There are five parts, known as titles, in the ADA, which we've summarized in Table 4.1.

SHRM Knowledge Domain(s): Workplace; Organization; Strategy
Functional Areas: U.S. Employment Law and Regulations, Risk Mngt., Business and HR Strategy, Employee Relations

The person has a physical or mental impairment that substantially limits one or more major life activities	The person has a record of such an impairment that substantially limits one or more major life activities; or	The person has been regarded by others as having such an impairment

Figure 4.2. ADA Definitions of a Disability

Table 4.1. Summary of the Five Titles in the ADA

ADA Title	Summary and Description
Title I—Employment	This prohibits discrimination of applicants and employees with disabilities, and also requires employers with 12–24 employees to provide reasonable accommodations that will level the playing field for people with disabilities and allow them to accomplish their work. Examples of accommodations include: • Modifying schedules • Restructuring jobs • Making the worksite more accessible
Title II—Public Services	State and local government agencies and employers that provide public services are prohibited from denying services to people with disabilities.
Title III—Public Accommodations	Requires owners of public commercial spaces to ensure that people with disabilities can enjoy those spaces.
Title IV—Telecommunications	Outlines that companies that provide phone service to the public provide a relay service for people with hearing and speech impairments.
Title V—Miscellaneous	This title covers a number of legal areas including prohibiting retaliation, coercion, or threats of people with disabilities or those helping them assert their rights in the ADA.

Getting Through the Process

The Society for Human Resource Management outlines the seven steps of going through an ADA accommodation process:

Step 1: Evaluate the Need for an Accommodation

• Determine if the employee believes performance of the essential functions of the job is possible, but reasonable accommodation is necessary to do so.

SHRM Knowledge Domain(s): Workplace; Organization; Strategy
Functional Areas: U.S. Employment Law and Regulations, Risk Mngt., Business and HR Strategy, Employee Relations

- An individual who decides to request accommodation must let the employer know—personally or through a representative—that an adjustment or change at work must be made for a reason related to a medical condition.
- Employers should be proactive in noticing when an employee's performance problems may be disability-related and in initiating discussions with the employee about whether an accommodation is necessary to performing the essential functions of the job.
- The ADA recognizes three categories of reasonable accommodations:

  1. Modifications or adjustments to a job application process
  2. Modifications or adjustments to the work environment or to the manner work is performed
  3. Modifications or adjustments that enable an employee with a disability to enjoy equal benefits and privileges of employment as are enjoyed by other similarly situated employees without disabilities.

Step 2: Understand Legal Rights and Responsibilities

- If the employee thinks an accommodation is necessary, the employer must determine whether the employee's condition qualifies as a protected disability under the ADA or under a comparable state law.
- Employers should understand that although they may be legally free to refuse an accommodation to individuals who are not covered under the law, employers are permitted to voluntarily do more for employees than the law requires and that doing so may be of benefit to the employer in a variety of ways.

Step 3: Conduct an Interactive Dialog on Reasonable Accommodation

- The employer must engage in an interactive process with the employee and, if necessary, with health care professionals to determine whether, as a matter of medical opinion, the employee can perform the essential functions of the job with or without a reasonable accommodation.

Step 4: Decide Whether Accommodations Are Reasonable

There are two things that an employer should consider in deciding if an accommodation is reasonable: undue hardship and direct threat.

- **Undue hardship.** The term refers not only to financial difficulty, but also to reasonable accommodations that are unduly extensive, substantial, or disruptive, or those that would fundamentally alter the nature or operation of the business.
- **Direct threat.** The ADA also allows an employer to refuse to hire, terminate, or demote an individual with a disability who poses a direct threat to the health or safety of other employees, customers, or the public.

Step 5: Consider Requiring a Health Examination

- If an employee provides insufficient information from a treating physician or other health care professional, an employer may require an individual to go to an appropriate health professional of the employer's choice to substantiate that the individual has an ADA disability and needs a reasonable accommodation.
- However, if an individual provides insufficient documentation in response to the employer's initial request, the employer should explain why the documentation is insufficient and allow the individual to provide the missing information in a timely manner.
- Documentation is insufficient if it does not specify the existence of an ADA disability or explain the need for reasonable accommodation.

Step 6: Select an Accommodation

- The employer may choose among reasonable accommodations, as long as the chosen accommodation is effective.
- An employer may offer alternative suggestions for reasonable accommodations and discuss their effectiveness in removing the workplace barrier impeding the disabled individual.

SHRM Knowledge Domain(s): Workplace; Organization; Strategy
Functional Areas: U.S. Employment Law and Regulations, Risk Mngt., Business and HR Strategy, Employee Relations

Step 7: Monitor and Document the Process

- The employer should closely monitor the situation to see whether the reasonable accommodation is indeed working. Is the employee now able to perform the essential functions of the job?
- If not, it may be necessary to go through Step 6 again to determine whether another reasonable accommodation would enable the employee to perform the essential functions of the job.

Understanding At-Will Employment

Some people believe that "at-will" employment allows a company to fire staff for anything and everything. It doesn't. In fact, employment-at-will is not a law at all, and it doesn't allow you to fire someone if you don't like them. Here's the deal: employment-at-will is a legal doctrine based on common law that gives both the employer and employee the ability to end the employment relationship at any time. There are some limitations on the employer side that can make firing someone illegal, such as violating federal and state discrimination statues based on an employee's race, color, religion, disability, sex, veteran status, or national origin.

Although many employers make it known that they are an at-will-employer in job applications, contracts, and offer letters, and require applicants to sign something that acknowledges the at-will relationship, some states protect employees from being fired for off-duty activities, marriage status, and physical appearance. Keep in mind that retaliation is a huge no-no, and there are both federal and state laws that prohibit employers from firing staff for doing things that are allowed by the law, like whistle-blowing, union activities, advocating for a minimum wage, or taking a stance on unlawful or discriminatory practices. A lot of these nuances vary by state labor laws, but there are three general exceptions (also see Table 4.2):

- Public Policy: These "represent a broad set of circumstances and vary from state to state." A good example is workers' compensation. It's a type of public policy, so many states prohibit employers from terminating an employee for filing a claim.

SHRM Knowledge Domain(s): Workplace; Organization; Strategy
Functional Areas: U.S. Employment Law and Regulations, Risk Mngt., Business and HR Strategy, Employee Relations

- Express or Implied Contracts: In some states, such as New Jersey, policies described in an employee handbook may be considered implied contracts. In others, such as Pennsylvania, the handbook may be seen simply as a set of guidelines, as opposed to binding policies.
- Good Faith: Recognized in 11 states, including California, this exception usually says that, in certain situations, employers can only dismiss employees for just cause. They also can't dismiss employees for reasons motivated by malice or made in bad faith.[8]

Having a signed acknowledgment of the at-will relationship is a great first step; however, it's also very important to document any and all performance related problems in the event your decision to let an employee go is challenged by a lawsuit claiming discrimination or other alleged legal violations.[9]

Table 4.2. At-Will Employment Exceptions

States WITHOUT Public Policy Exemptions	States that Do NOT Have Implied Contract Exemptions	States with Covenant of Good Faith Exemption
Alabama	Delaware	Alabama
Florida	Florida	Alaska
Georgia	Georgia	Arizona
Louisiana	Indiana	California
Nebraska	Louisiana	Delaware
New York	Massachusetts	Idaho
Rhode Island	Missouri	Massachusetts
	Montana	Montana
	North Carolina	Nebraska
	Pennsylvania	Utah
	Rhode Island	Wyoming
	Texas	
	Virginia	

RESOURCES, TEMPLATES, AND TOOLS FOR LEGAL, PART ONE
(Items in italics can be found in the appendix.)

FMLA
FMLA Affidavit of Family Relationship
FMLA Checklist for Individual Leave Request
FMLA Employee Request From
FMLA Employer Response (No Advance Notice)

FLSA
US Department of Labor, "Fair Labor Standards Act Adivsor," https://
    webapps.dol.gov/elaws/flsa.htm
FLSA Exemption Flow Chart
FLSA Exemption Questionnaire

ADA
ADA Communication to Employee in Response to Request for Accommodation
ADA Reasonable Accommodation Checklist
ADA Request for Reasonable Accommodation Form

At-Will Employment
Mark Feffer, "Employment at Will Isn't a Blank Check to
    Terminate Employees You Don't Like," https://www.shrm.
    org/resourcesandtools/hr-topics/employee-relations/pages/
    employment-at-will-isnt-a-blank-check-to-terminate-employees-
    you-dont-like.aspx

PART TWO: RISK MANAGEMENT, REGULATIONS, AND LABOR RELATIONS

Risk Assessment and Backup Planning

Startups and small businesses are well acquainted with risk. In fact, knowing when to take risks is an important part of any organization's success. However, the concept of risk management isn't often a thought or a priority. In this book, we define *risk management* as a set of deliberate steps business owners, officers, and managers take to prepare for interruptions to workflow and production. Interruptions can come from many angles, including funding, suppliers, and staff. We will focus on the interruptions to staffing, specifically how to prevent important information from walking out the door if and when someone who has that information leaves your company. A final focus will be creating a backup plan.

Make Sure to Give a NDA

Nondisclosure Agreements (NDAs) are legal documents created to help protect sensitive information, including trade secrets and proprietary information. This isn't something you want to create on your own, but should involve a qualified attorney that understands what the law allows without being too broad or in violation of federal employment protections. Once drafted correctly, a NDA can be given to newly hired staff and should be reviewed as part of the onboarding process. For employees already part of your company, consult an attorney about your state's requirements to make the agreement enforceable.

Avoid Having a Single Point of Failure

If your business relies on one person, place, or thing that is crucial to your operations, you have a single point of failure, a domino that if removed can be catastrophic to the survival of your company. This is where scenario planning can be vital to your risk management plan. Asking the questions in our Staffing Risk Management Planning Checklist can help in developing a backup plan. These might include things like training, shadowing, or mentoring, as well as developing manuals, guidebooks, or a process/how-to tool. See Exhibit 4.3 for the checklist.

Workers' Compensation

Small businesses need various types of insurance, and workers' compensation is one that should be part of your company's risk management strategy. If an employee gets injured or contracts a sickness on the job, workers' compensation can help protect your company and employees from financial losses. Although some states have different laws, most require private and public sector employers to have workers' compensation insurance. Texas is an exception and doesn't require workers' compensation, and those companies that choose not to have insurance in Texas risk being sued for work-related injuries. Federal employees are covered by different laws, and employees that telecommute and work remotely might be eligible for workers' compensation if they are injured while doing activities for their employment.

Every state allows employers to buy workers' compensation insurance to meet the requirement. Sometimes it can be tough for companies to find a private insurance company that will sell them insurance, especially companies with high risk activities and a history of high-cost claims. Some states allow companies to create, own, and operate employer-formed mutual insurance companies and employer-formed risk pools. Many small companies buy insurance for workers' compensation, and larger companies often self-fund. See Figure 4.3 for a summary of workers' compensation coverage purchasing options.

If an employee working for your company gets injured at work, regardless of who's at fault, the injured person is legally entitled to workers' compensation, and retaliation or discrimination against the injured person making a claim shouldn't happen. Injuries not covered are those that were purposely self-inflicted, obtained during an altercation that the employee started or when the employee was intoxicated, or psychological injuries without physical trauma. The good news is that employees can't sue your business for pain and suffering for work-related injuries or sickness. However, litigation can still happen if your company intentionally caused harm. Employers would be required to cover the cost of:

- Wage-loss benefits (a percentage of lost wages based on state calculations)
- Medical treatment (can be challenged by an employer to determine what's reasonable, if there are errors, or if the charges go above state standards)
- Rehabilitation treatment (therapeutic or education-based)
- Death benefits to family

Injured employees are entitled to family and medical leave of up to 12 weeks and, depending on the injury, reasonable accommodations discussed earlier in the chapter.

A successful workers' compensation process requires an understanding of your state's legal requirements, proactively ensuring that claims are work-related, keeping costs from snowballing out of control, and having genuine support and respect for the employee filing the claim. See Exhibit 4.4 for a workers' compensation risk management checklist.

State-Funded Workers' Compensation Program (more expensive)	Risk Pool—Group of Insurers that Share Coverage Risk (more expensive)	Employer-Formed Risk Pool (less expensive)

Employer-Formed Mutual Insurance Company (less expensive)	Self-Insure and Pay Claims via Third Party Claims Administrator (large-employer option)

Figure 4.3. Summary of Worker's Compensation Purchasing Options

Labor Management, Relations, and Unions

Labor relations in the United States have evolved around the issues of employee rights and fair employment standards over many years, and has led to the establishment of unions. Many small business owners worry about the impact union activities can have on their business, and wonder if anything can be done to prevent a union from forming. Keeping in mind that employees have a right to explore unionizing as an option, it might be helpful to think about what might lead your team to explore unionizing as an option:

• Feeling mistreated
• Poor working conditions
• Lack of communication between management and the team

Your company can minimize employee frustration and disappointment by building trust though good communication, open-door policies, fair and consistent policies, competitive pay, benefits, and recognition—all of which might discourage the belief in a need for a union.

It's possible that union organizing can still happen, even with the best employer-employee relationships. You as the employer should be aware of what you're allowed to do during that time. There are legal considerations and federal protections, and employers should not engage in the unfair labor practices outlined in Table 4.3. When there is a union, the U.S. Department of Labor enforces most of the provisions in the Labor-Management Reporting and Disclosure Act of 1959 (LMRDA). They provide a bill of rights for members of a union; give requirements for sharing financial information from labor unions, employers, and labor relations consultants when they are involved in certain activities; establish rules for creating and maintaining trusteeships; conduct elections for union officers; and create precautions for safeguarding union assets. Employees covered by the LMRDA work in private sector organizations or for the U.S. Postal Service.

The bottom line is that positive communication before, during, and after labor organizing activities is important for healthy labor relations. When communications break down in a unionized company, there is a possibility of a strike. There are certain strikes that are protected under the National Labor Relations Act (NLRA), which shields the rights of both employers and employees as it relates to business practices and the economy. Strikes that are allowed under the NLRA include:

- Unfair labor practice strikes, which protest an employer's illegal activities.
  - o Employers are allowed to hire replacement workers during this strike but cannot permanently replace those striking.
  - o Strikers are entitled to being reinstated.
- Economic strikes, which may occur when there are disputes over wages or benefits.
  - o Employers are allowed to hire replacement workers during this strike.
- Employees striking due to the company's inability to come to an agreement over pay or work conditions can be replaced but not terminated.
  - o Strikers are not entitled to reinstatement if they decide to return to work and positions are not available due to replacement workers being hired permanently.
  - o However, if strikers can't find equivalent employment elsewhere, they are entitled to be recalled as job openings become available.[10]

Table 4.3. Company Considerations During Union Activities

What You Can Do	What You Cannot Do
Hear out concerns	Threaten to terminate or reduce pay or benefits
Correspond with your employees	
Share your desire to stay union-free	Interrogate workers about their activities
Give the reasons you want to stay union-free	Promise anything, like benefits or promotions, for not joining the union
Inform employees of their right to not join a union	Spy on union meetings or pretend to spy
Provide information on the financial costs of joining a union	Punish employees through layoffs, terminations, or transfers to more difficult tasks
Share examples or stories on why unionizing might not be the right choice	

SHRM Knowledge Domain(s): Workplace; Organization; Strategy
Functional Areas: U.S. Employment Law and Regulations, Risk Mngt., Business and HR Strategy, Employee Relations

- Recognition strikes, which intend to force employers to recognize unions.
- Jurisdictional strikes, which are concerted refusals to work to affirm members' rights to particular job assignments and to protest the assignment of work to another union or to unorganized employees.[11]

A strike is unlawful and not covered by the NLRA when it violates a contract with a no-strike provision, there are agreements to use arbitration before a strike, the strike endangers the business property, or happens during a "cooling-off" period. Many states have their own laws regarding strikes. Seek out an attorney experienced with labor relations in small business settings to provide guidance on the specific challenges your company might be facing with labor relations. To learn more about federal labor relations, visit the U.S. Department of Labor website at www. dol.gov/general/topic/labor-relations.

RESOURCES, TEMPLATES, AND TOOLS FOR LEGAL, PART TWO
(Items in italics can be found in the appendix.)

Labor Relations
Allen Smith, "Complying with U.S. Labor Relations Laws in Non-Union Settings," https://www.shrm.org/ resourcesandtools/tools-and-samples/toolkits/pages/ lawsinnonunionsettings.aspx

Harassment
Investigation Summary Report Template
Retaliation Prevention Questionnaire

Workers' Compensation
Workers' Compensation Physician Designation

Unions
Union-Free Policy

SHRM Knowledge Domain(s): Workplace; Organization; Strategy
Functional Areas: U.S. Employment Law and Regulations, Risk Mngt., Business and HR Strategy, Employee Relations

ADDITIONAL TOOLS

Table 4.4. The FMLA Employee Eligibility Checklist

Requirement	Description	Yes	No
A covered employer	Is your company a covered employer? The Department of Labor requires that public agencies, schools, and private sector employers with 50 or more employees with at least 20 work weeks in the current or prior calendar year provide family and medical leave. Visit www.dol.gov/whd.	☐	☐
Number of hours worked	Has the employee worked 1,250 hours during the previous 12 months before the family and medical leave start date?	☐	☐
Work location	Does the employee work at a location that has 50 or more employees within 75 miles?	☐	☐
Months employed	Has the employee worked for your company for 12 months? These do not need to be consecutive months.	☐	☐

© *Copyright 2020 by Marie Carasco*

Table 4.5. FMLA-Covered Circumstances and Leave Time

Leave Entitlement	Circumstances	Description
12 Weeks	Birth of or bonding with a child	Caring for a newborn child within the first year of birth. Both mothers and fathers are eligible.
	Placement with a child	Placement with an adopted child, fostering, or other child placed in the employee's care.
	Caring for ill family	Caring for an employee's ill parent, spouse, or child with a serious health-related condition.
	Covered military situation	Circumstances that emerge from an employee's parent, spouse, or child with covered military service.
26 Weeks	Ill or injured military family	Caring for an employee's ill or injured next of kin, parent, spouse, or child with covered military service (military caregiver leave).

REFERENCES

"Americans with Disabilities Act (ADA)." In *Encyclopedia of Small Business*, 4th ed., edited by Virgil L. Burton, III, 56–60. Vol. 1. Detroit, MI: Gale, 2011. Gale Virtual Reference Library.

Society for Human Resource Management. "Accommodating Employees' Disabilities." Accessed May 20, 2019. https://www.shrm.org/resourcesandtools/tools-and-samples/toolkits/pages/accommodatingdisabilities.aspx.

Society for Human Resource Management. "Employment at Will Isn't a Blank Check to Terminate Employees You Don't Like." Accessed May 22, 2019. https://www.shrm.org/resourcesandtools/hr-topics/employee-relations/pages/employment-at-will-isnt-a-blank-check-to-terminate-employees-you-dont-like.aspx.

Society for Human Resource Management. "FMLA Compliance Checklist." Accessed May 20, 2019. https://www.shrm.org/ResourcesAndTools/tools-and-samples/hr-forms/Pages/familyandmedicalleaveact(fmla)checklist.aspx.

Society for Human Resource Management. "What Is Meant by the Terms 'Exempt', 'Non-Exempt', 'Salaried' and 'Hourly'?" Accessed May 20, 2019. https://www.shrm.org/resourcesandtools/tools-and-samples/hr-qa/pages/whatismeantbythetermsexempt,non-exempt,salariedandhourly.aspx.

Society for Human Resource Management. "What Should Employers Do When Workers Exhaust FMLA Leave." Accessed May 20, 2019. https://www.shrm.org/resourcesandtools/legal-and-compliance/employment-law/pages/workers-exhaust-fmla-leave.aspx.

U.S. Department of Labor. "FMLA Frequently Asked Questions." Accessed May 20, 2019. https://www.dol.gov/whd/fmla/fmla-faqs.htm.

U.S. Department of Labor. "Summary of the Major Laws of the Department of Labor." Accessed May 20, 2019. https://www.dol.gov/general/aboutdol/majorlaws.

ENDNOTES

1. " FMLA Frequently Asked Questions," U.S. Department of Labor, accessed May 20, 2019, https://www.dol.gov/whd/fmla/fmla-faqs.htm.

2. "What Should Employers Do When Workers Exhaust FMLA Leave," accessed May 20, 2019, https://www.shrm.org/resourcesandtools/legal-and-compliance/employment-law/pages/workers-exhaust-fmla-leave.aspx.

3. "FMLA Frequently Asked Questions," U.S. Department of Labor, accessed May 20, 2019, https://www.dol.gov/whd/fmla/fmla-faqs.htm.

4. "What is meant by the terms 'exempt', 'non-exempt', 'salaried' and 'hourly'?", SHRM, accessed May 20, 2019, https://www.shrm.org/resourcesandtools/tools-and-samples/hr-qa/pages/whatismeantbythetermsexempt,non-exempt,salariedandhourly.aspx.

5. "Summary of the Major Laws of the Department of Labor," U.S. Department of Labor, accessed May 20, 2019, https://www.dol.gov/general/aboutdol/majorlaws.

6. "Accommodating Employees' Disabilities", SHRM, accessed May 20, 2019, https://www.shrm.org/resourcesandtools/tools-and-samples/toolkits/pages/accommodating disabilities.aspx.

7. "Americans with Disabilities Act (ADA)," Encyclopedia of Small Business, accessed May 20, 2019, http://link.galegroup.com.libproxy.utdallas.edu/apps/doc/CX2343700030/GVRL?u=txshracd2602&sid=GVRL&xid=ed9e62aa. Accessed 20 May 2019.

8. "Accommodating Employees' Disabilities," SHRM, accessed May 20, 2019, https://www.shrm.org/resourcesandtools/tools-and-samples/toolkits/pages/accommodating disabilities.aspx.

9. "Employment at Will Isn't a Blank Check to Terminate Employees You Don't Like," SHRM, accessed May 22, 2019, https://www.shrm.org/resourcesandtools/hr-topics/employee-relations/pages/employment-at-will-isnt-a-blank-check-to-terminate-employees-you-dont-like.aspx.

10. "Are all types of strikes protected under the National Labor Relations Act?," SHRM, accessed May 28, 2019, https://www.shrm.org/resourcesandtools/tools-and-samples/hr-qa/pages/cms_021003.aspx.

11. "Are All Types of Strikes Protected under the National Labor Relations Act?," SHRM, accessed May 28, 2019, https://www.shrm.org/resourcesandtools/tools-and-samples/hr-qa/pages/cms_021003.aspx.

12. "FMLA Compliance Checklist," SHRM, accessed May 20, 2019, https://www.shrm.org/ResourcesAndTools/tools-and-samples/hr-forms/Pages/familyandmedical leaveact(fmla)checklist.aspx.

Exhibit 4.1. FMLA Compliance Checklist

GENERAL[12]

[ ] Is the employer covered by the FMLA?

[ ] Is the FMLA poster displayed in an area frequented by employees and applicants?

[ ] Is there a written FMLA policy included in the employee handbook or otherwise distributed?

[ ] Is the 12-month period used to calculate FMLA leave defined in the written policy?

[ ] Is there a method for tracking employee use of family and medical leave and remaining leave entitlement?

[ ] Have the FMLA forms from the U.S. Department of Labor been downloaded, or have similar internal forms been created? See www.dol.gov/whd/fmla/forms.htm.

[ ] Is training provided to managers on the FMLA, including information about how to identify a leave request that may be FMLA-qualifying and how to comply with anti-retaliation rules?

[ ] Are procedures in place and communicated to employees regarding requests for family and medical leave and the consequences of failing to provide proper notice?

LEAVE REQUESTS

[ ] Is the employee's request for leave due to an FMLA-qualifying reason?

[ ] Is the employee eligible for family and medical leave?

[ ] Is the Notice of Eligibility and Rights and Responsibilities form (WH-381) provided within five days of learning of the need for leave that may be FMLA-qualifying?

[ ] Is a medical certification necessary? If yes:

[ ] Is the appropriate certification form provided to the employee?

[ ] Is the employee given at least 15 calendar days to return the certification form?

[ ] Are the consequences for not returning the certification form communicated?

(continued)

[] Is the certification form returned completely and sufficiently without missing information or sections left blank or vague?

[] Is the employee given at least seven days to submit a corrected certification form, if necessary?

[] Is the Designation Notice (WH-382) provided within five days of receipt of the medical certification?

[] If no medical certification is required, is the employee provided with the Designation Notice (WH-382) with the Notice of Eligibility and Rights and Responsibility form (WH-381) within five days of learning of the need for family and medical leave?

[] Are key employees identified and notified of their status as such with an explanation of their limited reinstatement rights?

DURING LEAVE

[] Is coverage under the group health plan maintained at the same level and under the same conditions as would be maintained had the employee not taken leave, including employer contributions?

[] Is there a process to collect premium payments for health insurance from employees during periods of unpaid family and medical leave?

[] Do internal policies indicate how other benefits are impacted by a family and medical leave absence, such as paid-time-off accruals, life insurance, etc.?

[] Are requirements for the employee to provide periodic updates to the employer during leave communicated?

RETURN TO WORK

[] Is a release to work from a health care provider required before returning to work?

[] Is the employee reinstated to the same or an equivalent position?

[] Is there a process to collect outstanding insurance premiums owed by the employee?

[] Are records of the employee's family and medical leave retained for a minimum of three years, separate from the employee's personnel file?

Reprinted with permission. ©Society for Human Resource Management.

SHRM Knowledge Domain(s): Workplace; Organization; Strategy
Functional Areas: U.S. Employment Law and Regulations, Risk Mngt., Business and HR Strategy, Employee Relations

Exhibit 4.2. FLSA Compliance Checklist

GENERAL

[ ] Is the employer covered by the FLSA?

[ ] Are the federal and state minimum wage requirements followed?

[ ] Who is exempt from minimum wage and overtime pay? (Note that executives are exempt.) Visit www.dol.gov/whd.

[ ] Are minors under 16 restricted from hazardous conditions and working too many hours?

[ ] Is every covered employee being paid for all hours worked in a work week?

[ ] Is overtime being paid at time-and-a-half of the employee's regular rate for each hour worked?

[ ] Are those necessary informed that retaliation for filing complaints is prohibited by law?

[ ] Is a filing system that meets the requirements of the U.S. Department of Labor in place?

RECORD KEEPING GUIDANCE FOR MINIMUM WAGE EMPLOYEES

[ ] Is the employee name, home address, occupation, gender, and birthdate (if under 19) in the file?

[ ] Have the hour and day when the work begins been added to the file?

[ ] What are the total hours worked for each work day in the work week?

[ ] What are the total daily or weekly straight-time earnings?

[ ] What is the regular hourly pay rate for any week when overtime is worked?

[ ] What is the total overtime pay for the workweek?

[ ] What are the deductions from additional wages earned?

[ ] What are the total wages paid each pay period?

[ ] What is the date of payment and pay period covered?

(continued)

SHRM Knowledge Domain(s): Workplace; Organization; Strategy
Functional Areas: U.S. Employment Law and Regulations, Risk Mngt., Business and HR Strategy, Employee Relations

NURSING MOTHERS

[ ] Is a reasonable break time provided for an employee to express breast milk? This applies to companies with 50 or more employees.

[ ] Do we have a private space (not a bathroom) that is functional, free from intrusion, shielded from view of coworkers and the public, and available for expressing breast milk when needed?

© *Copyright 2020 by Marie Carasco*

Exhibit 4.3. Staffing Risk Management Planning Checklist

GENERAL

[ ] Has time been scheduled with an attorney to draft a Non-Disclosure Agreement (NDA)?

[ ] Are the NDAs given to new hires and current staff?

[ ] Are the NDAs reviewed during the onboarding process?

[ ] Have scenario plans on what can go wrong been created?

[ ] What would happen if [most important person to business] leaves?

[ ] Do we know enough about what [most important person to business] accomplishes for the business to survive in their absence?

[ ] What are three things that can be done in the next three, six, and nine months to ensure that someone else learns what [most important person to business] knows?

[ ] What is being tolerated from [most important person to business] because of the value they bring to the business that shouldn't be?

[ ] Is there a backup plan that can act as a guide on what to do if things go wrong?

[ ] Has someone trustworthy outside of the company been identified who can help pinpoint other risks that haven't been considered?

© *Copyright 2020 by Marie Carasco*

SHRM Knowledge Domain(s): Workplace; Organization; Strategy
Functional Areas: U.S. Employment Law and Regulations, Risk Mngt., Business and HR Strategy, Employee Relations

Exhibit 4.4. Workers' Compensation Risk Management Checklist
GENERAL

[] Have frequent sources of injuries and illnesses been identified?

[] Repetitive actions

[] Lifting and bending

[] Pinching

[] Machinery _____

[] Falls

[] Environmental exposure

[] Psychological trauma

[] Where can risk and liability be avoided?

[] Are there operations that do not require employees?

[] What high-risk activities can be outsourced?

_____

[] What work with risks of injuries can be taken on entirely by a contractor?

_____

[] Have supervisors been educated?

[] How does information on workplace injuries and the workers' compensation process get shared? Is there an employee handbook or new hire orientation?

MANAGING CLAIMS

[] Is the injury work-related?

[] Is the employee unable to work?

[] Is the medical treatment necessary?

[] Are the medical records needed to process the claims available?

[] How are medical records kept confidential?

SHRM Knowledge Domain(s): Workplace; Organization; Strategy
Functional Areas: U.S. Employment Law and Regulations, Risk Mngt., Business and HR Strategy, Employee Relations

[ ] Is a rapport being developed with the medical doctor(s)? This includes providing enough information to make an informed decision, such as the job description.

[ ] Are there reasons to challenge a claim?

[ ] Is there evidence that the employee is not disabled?

[ ] Does a private investigator need to be hired?

RETURNING TO WORK

[ ] What can be done to assist the employee's return to work as soon as possible?

[ ] What light duty, supervised, or transitional work can be done?

[ ] What workplace accommodations can be made?

[ ] Is a record being kept of the scheduled return dates to follow-up if the employee does not show up when expected?

[ ] Are preparations made to let the employee go (with the advice of an attorney) if they refuse to return to work when they should?

SHRM Knowledge Domain(s): Workplace; Organization; Strategy
Functional Areas: U.S. Employment Law and Regulations, Risk Mngt., Business and HR Strategy, Employee Relations

CHAPTER 5

Planning for the Future (Assuming You Survive the Now)

William J. Rothwell

QUICK-START GUIDE TO PLANNING FOR THE FUTURE

Chapter Five in a Nutshell

If you have a long-term vision and goals to grow your company, you need a strategic workforce plan to make it happen.[1]

To do so, you will need to:

- Understand how many people are needed in the future to achieve the organization's strategic goals and how to close any gaps
- Develop your key people to meet their present work and job requirements, keep their skills updated, and prepare them for future work and job requirements
- Know the strengths and talents demonstrated by the people in your organization
- Leverage your company's competitive advantages based on your employees' talents and organization innovation
- Use the right data and analytics to forecast your decision-making

This chapter focuses on these areas and other related topics.

Planning For Growth: Strategic Workforce Planning
Business Case and Lessons Learned

Dana Samuelson is president of Maya Pharmacy, a compound pharmacy in New Mexico that produces custom-made medicines. Dana founded her pharmacy in 1990 when she received her New Mexico pharmacist license and quit her job at Walgreens. Dana had friends who were doing small-scale medicine production, so she went into business with them to create specialized lotions, ointments, and other medical compounds.

Her pharmacy now employs 20 people on one shift who work 40 hours per week. The business generates a net profit of over $1 million per year despite being valued at only $4 million. Dana knows she has been blessed with such success. She keeps her head down and simply makes medicines without advertising the profitability of her business.

SHRM Knowledge Domain(s): Organization; Strategy
Functional Areas: Workforce Management; Business & HR Strategy

As her store grew, Dana did very little to plan for staffing needs. When she noticed her workers getting overwhelmed, she would simply ask them if they needed help. If they said they did, Dana would use the old-fashioned approach of putting an advertisement in the newspaper and hoping that it would surface qualified job applicants. Workers were hired based on their resumés, and there wasn't much effort to check their backgrounds. However, given the nature of the business, Dana learned the hard way that she had to do criminal background checks on workers because she could ill afford to employ people with any history of drug arrests or convictions.

Dana wants to grow her business and add stores to make more medicines, but she's not in a rush. She wants to get it right, so she hired a consultant to help her conduct strategic workforce planning. Dana wants to bring more order to the chaotic way her business has grown. She thinks there must be a better way to plan for the right quantity and quality of staff, rather than just asking people if they need help and then seeking out suitable applicants. In particular, she wants to make sure her staff align with the long-term direction of the business.

The consultants began their work by conducting a *Delphi process*. It is a way of forecasting needs based on information gathered from several rounds of questionnaires or panel discussions, in this case with the four managers in the pharmacy. The consultants asked them to provide the names, detailed job descriptions, and measurable results of their workers. They also asked for the job titles and salary levels of all employees. By compiling that information, the consultants obtained a benchmark of the possible productivity levels by a pharmacy of the same size and staffing level.

Lessons Learned

- When strategic growth is a priority, it is necessary to take the time to understand exactly the kind of roles and skills needed to meet the growth needs.
- Looking inside your company and understanding the skills and abilities which make your best people successful can give your business a competitive edge to benchmark and evaluate future hires.

SHRM Knowledge Domain(s): Organization; Strategy
Functional Areas: Workforce Management; Business & HR Strategy

Every growing business will inevitably need to think about the short- and long-term staffing needs for their organizations. That means they must think about *strategic workforce* planning, a process of identifying the quantity and quality of people needed by an organization over time to achieve its strategic, competitive goals.[2] Stated another way, strategic workforce planning answers the question:"How many and what kind of people are needed by my organization over time to achieve our strategic goals?" It also asks:"How can we create a culture of inclusion? How do we plan staff development and progression? How do we identify talented people for future leadership, know how many people we need, and use the right data for successful implementation plans like this?"This chapter address these important questions.

PLANNING FOR STAFF DEVELOPMENT AND PROGRESSION

Who hasn't heard the phrase, "people are our most important asset." If they are, then small business leaders should demonstrate support for staff development. (*Talent development* is the popular term used today.) But the real test is whether resources match rhetoric. How much money and time does the organization devote to *development* (meaning the continuing process to help people meet their present work and job requirements), keep their skills updated amid changing and dynamic working conditions, and prepare for future work and job requirements? Development prepares people for *career progression*, or "forward career movement." It equips them for more responsibility by demonstrating a deeper or broader grasp of their occupational skills and specializations, or some combination of any or all of those methods.

Using Competencies to Plan for Staff Development

One form of development is *competency-based staff development* (or *competency-based training*), a system that bases development on a researched profile of the present and/or future ideal worker.[3] Instead of focusing on job descriptions, which are often dated and incomplete, a competency-based system centers on making people successful at the work they do by studying people who are successful. A college degree is not required for

job success; in fact, a competency-based system is neither time-based
nor knowledge-based. Instead, it's based on performance requirements. Workers focus on learning how to get results and demonstrate
that achievement. Feedback on learner performance is more frequent
and more specific than in traditional education and training. There is
also more learner assessment, which compares individual achievement
to the behavioral competency requirements linked to job success based
on research studies. Learners must show what they can do rather than
pass paper-and-pencil tests.

Defining Competencies
Competencies are individual characteristics that serve as the foundation for successful or outstanding job performance.[4] They can also be
described by level, functional, or technical areas on the organization
chart, and can center on issues that are diagonal, cross-sectional slices
across levels and silos. Performance is judged by behaviors and work
results. Competency-based learning aims to help learners demonstrate
necessary behaviors and give evidence that they can produce needed
work results.

Competencies connect individual requirements to organizational
requirements, and can help to organize development. Since each job
requires the demonstration of competencies, competency-building is
necessary to qualify for a job, remain current in the job, and qualify for
career progression into future jobs.

Identifying Competencies
There are three ways to identify competencies.[5] The first is by borrowing competency models from other, usually similar, organizations. As an
example, a bank might rely on competency models taken from other
banks or from banking associations. A second way is by borrowing and
modifying competencies from similar organizations. This is a tailoring
process. A third way is to identify competencies through qualitative and
quantitative research. This will take constraints of time and money, so
consider looking into the first two options. Competencies are identified

using Behavioral Event Interviews, where critical incidents (stories) are collected through an interview process.[6]

IDENTIFYING TOP TALENT FOR LEADERSHIP

Leaders are among the first people to be chosen when organizations are launched. Often, those who enter the organization in its early days are promoted from within as it grows. For that reason, early decisions about who to hire will affect the organization for many years as workers are transformed into leaders.

One way to conceptualize top talent is to think of *key people* or *key positions*. A *key person* is an individual who is critical to the organization's operations. The loss of that person would have an outsized (and usually negative) impact on business operations. A *key position* is a spot on the organization chart that is critical to the organization's operations. A key position is all about the strategic nature of the job; a key person is all about the strategic value of the *job incumbent*, the person performing the job.

Identifying Key People

How does the organization identify key people and/or key positions as part of strategic workforce planning? Start by asking decision makers which individuals are most important in getting business results. Whose sudden, unexpected loss would be most disruptive and counterproductive to business operations? Which individuals in the organization are perhaps best-known for their business or industry knowledge, innovation, creativity, or reputation, and their social relationships with customers, suppliers, distributors, government regulators, union representatives, news media, and other important stakeholders? The answers to those questions would indicate the key people.

Key people are not just those topping the organization chart. Indeed, as one example, universities would be unable to function effectively without secretaries and staff assistants. The same principle applies to other organizations. Sometimes key people reside several levels down on an organization chart, but they are important nevertheless! Examine the tool at the end of this chapter to gather critical information about key people.

SHRM Knowledge Domain(s): Organization; Strategy
Functional Areas: Workforce Management; Business & HR Strategy

More on Identifying Key People

To identify key positions, start by looking at the organization chart. Who is at the top of the organization chart? Who is at the top of each function, division, or department? Who is at the top of each work group or team? Anyone at the top of these locations on the organization chart occupies a key position.

It is difficult to imagine most organizations functioning well if they lost their chief executive officer. Ships will crash on the shore if no captain is steering the ship, and the same principle applies to organizations. Yet, it can take a lot of time to recruit well-qualified senior leaders. Knowing what they bring to the company makes it easier to plan for their unexpected loss. Examine the tool at the end of this chapter to gather critical information about job incumbents in key positions.

Why Is It Important to Identify Key People and/or Key Positions?

Identifying key people and/or key positions is important in strategic workforce planning. The word *key* suggests a person or position who is qualitatively important to the organization or business. Once these individuals or positions are identified, then it just makes sense to reflect on what to do in case of the sudden, unexpected loss of key people or those in key positions.[7]

Decision-makers often associate replacing people or position incumbents with HR actions, like recruiting from outside the organization or promoting from inside the organization. However, great care should be taken with such simplistic solutions. When the organization loses a key person or a job incumbent in a key position, the real question is *"How can the work be performed with quality?,"* not *"Who can fill the vacancy?"* The goal is to get the work done and not fill a position. When the problem is framed in this way, it opens up more solutions than simply recruiting from outside the organization or internal promotions. There are over 100 possible ways to get work done.[8] Some of those solutions include automating, eliminating, outsourcing, or offshoring the work, as well as reassigning the work to a team rather than an individual, combining jobs, or hiring contingent workers to perform the job.

SHRM Knowledge Domain(s): Organization; Strategy
Functional Areas: Workforce Management; Business & HR Strategy

UNDERSTANDING YOUR LABOR SUPPLY AND DEMAND

Strategic workforce planning is a continual process of identifying the human resources needed to achieve organizational goals, and finding or developing people to achieve those goals. Few organizations use systematic, strategic workforce planning to bring labor supply and demand into balance in the present or for the future. A more common approach is to add people or positions as vacancies occur, or else as the organization's leaders experience "felt needs" that staff should be added. Another approach is to correctively find ways to get work done—perhaps using the strategies described in the previous section of this chapter. Neither approach is *strategic* workforce planning; rather, it is *ad hoc* (meaning "on the fly" or "shooting from the hip") workforce planning.

Strategic workforce planning requires addressing the following important questions:

- *How many people does the organization employ at present?*
  This question centers around labor supply but focuses on the quantity of people. What is the organization headcount? How many people work in each department, and how does that relate to workload? Overtime? Any other key issues? What does the current labor force cost, and what revenue is generated by that labor force?

- *What kind of people does the organization employ at present?*
  This question centers around labor supply but focuses on the quality of people. What competencies do the managers and workers possess? What is the educational level of the workforce? What is the reputation of the people who work in the organization? How is each department configured by competency levels? How many in-house experts are employed by the organization at present?

- *How many people are needed in the future to achieve the organization's strategic goals?*
  What headcount is needed in the future to meet the productivity and other goals of the organization? What labor budget is expected in the future? What is the relationship between headcount/cost and work outputs?

- *What kind of people are needed in the future to achieve the organization's strategic goals?*
  This question centers around labor supply but focuses on the quality of the people needed to achieve long-term goals. What competencies do the managers and workers need to possess in the future? What educational levels will be needed for the workforce of the future? How should each department be configured by competency-levels in the future to realize strategic goals? How many in-house experts will be needed by the organization over time?

- *What are the present gaps between labor supply and labor demand?*
  What gaps exist between present labor supply (quantity and quality) and present labor demand (quantity and quality)?

- *What are the future gaps between labor supply and labor demand?*
  If no decided action is taken between the present and future, what gaps will exist in the future between supply and demand?

- *How can gaps between present labor supply and present labor demand be closed?*

- *What HR steps should be taken now to close gaps between present labor supply and demand?*
  For instance, who should be recruited, selected, onboarded, trained, promoted, and transferred? What percentage of the labor force should consist of so-called full-time workers and what percentage should consist of such alternatives as contingent workers, consultants, outsourced labor, and so forth?

- *How can gaps between present and future labor supply and present and future labor demand be closed?*
  What HR steps should be taken over time to close gaps between labor supply and demand? For instance, who should be recruited, selected, onboarded, trained, promoted, and transferred? What percentage of the labor force should consist of so-called full-time workers over time and what percentage should consist of such alternatives as contingent workers, consultants, outsourced labor, and so forth over time?

SHRM Knowledge Domain(s): Organization; Strategy
Functional Areas: Workforce Management; Business & HR Strategy

- *How can the success of closing present and future gaps be evaluated?*
  What metrics should be used to evaluate the relative success of identifying and taking steps to close gaps between present and future labor supply and demand? How can the contribution of the workforce plan in achieving the organization's strategic goals be measured?

This is a lot of work, and requires careful planning to get it done well—remember that "the talent of people comes first and organizational strategy comes second, building on those talents."

If this new logic is added to the old, then it is important to add some additional questions to the strategic workforce questions listed above:

- What talents are demonstrated by people in the organization?
- How many people have what kind of talents?
- What competitive advantages can be leveraged based on the talents and innovation of the organization's people?

As the world's economy moves from information-based to innovation-based, talent-based thinking becomes more important. Labor is still regarded as a "cost of doing business" rather than as the source of innovation that cannot be replaced easily by land, capital, or technology. But without talented labor, there would be no new organizations founded by entrepreneurs. Without a continuing influx of talented labor, no organization would exist for long because there would be no human agency to use capital, land, or technology.

Strategic workforce planning makes it possible for leaders to discuss how many and what kind of people are needed to achieve organizational goals. Doing that is just as important as discussing how much and what kind of capital is needed, or how much and what kind of technology is needed. Unfortunately, while many senior managers pay lip service to HR, far fewer actually spend as much time planning for people as they do planning for sourcing funding or technology. That signals a difference in values about what is really important.

SHRM Knowledge Domain(s): Organization; Strategy
Functional Areas: Workforce Management; Business & HR Strategy

The best time to conduct systematic, strategic workforce planning is at the same time, or immediately following, the strategic planning process for the business. While the HR department may take the lead in facilitating discussions about workforce plans, it is important to emphasize that managing people is an issue owned by all managers—not just by HR. Leaders have a daily role in building talent.[9]

CONDUCTING EFFECTIVE, STRATEGIC WORKFORCE PLANNING

If the organization aims to apply strategic workforce planning successfully and systematically, an organized approach is essential. Some organizations establish a department focused on workforce planning; some make a department tasked with facilitating strategic planning responsible; and some assign the duty to a standing task force, council, or committee. If your business has the time and resources, the best place to start workforce planning would be with a committee. Or, simply gather your best thinkers across the company, those who would take this process seriously, and designate a time for everyone to get together and make it happen. It can be a good way to build understanding of workforce planning among managers. Here's a short list of the key things to get it going:

- Identify the person with the HR responsibility as the leader of the team
- Get a senior executive to serve as a change champion for the effort
- Find ways to build involvement and understanding of workforce planning with the managers
- Carry out the steps identified above with the group
- Make sure that workforce planning provides useful information that can be used to inform organizational strategic plans and HR actions
- Find ways to evaluate the workforce plan over time that won't feel like a waste of time

SHRM Knowledge Domain(s): Organization; Strategy
Functional Areas: Workforce Management; Business & HR Strategy

LEVERAGING DATA ANALYTICS FOR
SUCCESSFUL IMPLEMENTATION

Data, data, everywhere, especially big data. There's something to be said for all the information and trends out there, being used to help companies make decisions that may shift the direction and resources in their business. It shouldn't surprise you that an emerging trend in HR is to focus on workforce statistics.[10] Using data analytics can help your organization's leaders pinpoint important issues affecting recruitment, selection, onboarding, training, development, appraisals, management, rewards, and retention. "HR analytics" are used for successful implementation of HR strategies, such as strategic workforce planning. Popular HR analytics include:

- *Turnover rate:* Calculated by dividing number of voluntary quits over total headcount, multiplied by 100
- *Absenteeism rate:* Calculated by dividing number of missing workers per day over total headcount, multiplied by 100 (absenteeism is predictive of turnover)
- *Critical turnover:* Calculated by dividing number of high potential workers quits over total headcount of high potentials, multiplied by 100. (This number is important because high potentials may be as much as 20 times more productive than average performers.)
- *Comparison of percentage of external hires to internal promotions:* Divide number of external hires by total headcount, then multiply by 100; divide number of internal promotions by total headcount, then multiply by 100. Finally, compare the two percentages. In volatile industries, it is not unusual to hire 80 percent of employees externally, compared to 20 percent by internal promotions. In stable industries—government is the best example—it is not unusual to see 80 percent of positions filled by internal promotions and only 20 percent filled by external hires.
- *Hit rate:* Percentage of workers listed on succession plans who are actually promoted when vacancies occur.

The real questions are:

- Which statistics are useful?
- Which statistics are worth taking time to collect, analyze, and act upon?

DEVELOPING AN INCLUSIVE WORKPLACE

What is an inclusive workplace? How does an inclusive workplace relate to strategic workforce planning? How can such a workplace be established? This section addresses these questions.

Defining the Inclusive Workplace

According to Esther Mollema's book, *Success in Managing Diversity,* the word *inclusiveness* is defined by adherence to six key issues, where leaders are:[11]

- Open to all ideas.
- Open to all actions.
- Encouraging openness.
- Encouraging open-mindedness regarding all new ideas.
- Remaining tenacious in their actions and demonstrating confidence.
- Encouraging individuals to realize their potential.

Leaders who can build and sustain a climate supportive of inclusiveness must demonstrate unique characteristics.[12] Inclusiveness is a value system. It's about how people behave—and how their leaders encourage them to behave. What leaders say and do are keys to the success of an inclusive system. Leaders model inclusiveness in both word and deed by adhering to the values listed above. Inclusive leaders avoid defensiveness and are authentic in what they say and do, which is appreciated by their staff. These leaders are not paralyzed by criticism, but are open to new thoughts and new views. They are willing to explore new innovations, realizing that business breakthroughs come from the exercise of simple curiosity. Inclusive leaders do not shut down ideas simply because they do not match up to traditional thinking or to the leaders' personal preferences. They are relentlessly determined to find new ways and encourage others to develop themselves as well as their ideas.

How an Inclusive Workplace Relates to Strategic Workforce Planning

Most of the time, folks in HR look at workforce planning as a process of deciding how many people (headcount) and what kind of people (competencies) are needed by an organization. Sometimes that takes the related view of how many people (by cost) lead to how much productivity (sales generated). This traditional view of workplace planning focuses solely on the quantity and quality of workers—or their costs compared to the revenues they generate.

Yet, inclusiveness is about the relative openness of the company culture to diversity in thinking, doing, and being. It also means paying attention to values and not just the quantities and qualities of the staff. Inclusive cultures give more attention to innovation because they are less restrictive than traditional businesses.[13] Currently, many business observers believe the competitive future belongs to organizations that are more innovative than others.[14]

Establishing an Inclusive Workplace

How can inclusiveness be encouraged? The answer, while it sounds simple, is really quite profound—the organization's leaders must be deliberate in building a culture of inclusiveness. Building that culture from the organization's origin, or green site, is easier than trying to convert an ingrained (brown site) culture to new thinking. Business founders must encourage inclusiveness from the outset and select people for leadership who demonstrate the behaviors associated with inclusiveness. Workers follow their leaders, and the founders' views are crucial for setting the right example and creating the foundation for stories that dramatically illustrate the work culture. Stories, after all, carry the culture.

To establish the right foundations for an inclusive culture, leaders should ensure that the values of inclusiveness are embodied in human resource policies, procedures, and practices. To start, try taking a pulse check by pulling together a team from across the company and seeing how well the organization encourages inclusiveness in recruiting, selecting, onboarding, training, managing performance, and promoting people. The team should first examine what is written about inclusiveness in the policies and manuals. The next step is to pinpoint areas for improvement regarding inclusiveness and brainstorm methods of refinement. The organization's leaders should demonstrate their commitment by getting involved with the teams and featuring inclusiveness in exit interview questions. Training all staff members can help encourage an inclusive culture, but it should never be the only method. Pulse checks can be done annually to help maintain an inclusive culture.

BALANCING INCLUSION AND ACCOMMODATION

Diversity and Inclusion Business Case and Lessons Learned

Patrick Bardsley, CEO and co-founder of Spectrum Designs Foundation, runs a social enterprise that employs people with disabilities, particularly autism. It's not just a place to get a paycheck, but a place to help individuals with autism lead full and productive lives through the world of work. Spectrum Designs Foundation was intentional in establishing five core values from the beginning: people, professionalism, health, innovation, and mission. These values have become the lens from which they foster diversity and inclusion for everyone that joins the company.

The Hiring Process

Spectrum Designs Foundation hires people that are differently able or with autism, and others without. They revamped and reshaped their interview questions around the organization's five core values so that they could evaluate and receive insight on how candidates felt about the work environment. They now ask questions like "How do you feel when walking in here?" and "What do you think of the mission of the organization?" The new hire has to fit with the culture because it can be challenging to maintain a balanced level of inclusion for all staff. For example, all staff are invited to join events. However, it's up to the employee to decide and discuss personal involvement with the event. Spectrum Designs Foundation wants to be sure that people who join the company can navigate situations where a staff

(continued)

SHRM Knowledge Domain(s): Organization; Strategy
Functional Areas: Workforce Management; Business & HR Strategy

member might feel overwhelmed by stimulus, or when they're not sure how they want to interact within a particular setting.

Taking a Non-Traditional Approach to Assessment

Patrick highlighted that Spectrum Designs Foundation has been trying to move away from traditional interviews in some cases. They favor more practical assessments of people's skills by having candidates actually perform the work they would do if hired. That's because, in Patrick's opinion, sitting across from someone and having a 45-minute conversation about that person does not provide a fair assessment of the candidate's skills.

Over time, the team has learned one of its biggest lessons from the hiring process—if they find someone who is passionate; understands their "why"; and represents the culture, inclusiveness, and diversity values of the company, it's easier to hire that person and teach them skills than to hire someone who's very talented but doesn't represent the culture.

Navigating Accommodations

An organization like Spectrum Designs Foundation requires a careful balance. The challenge is in making sure that everyone's held to the same standards, which can be difficult when you have varying levels of ability. An example would be the professionalism core value. Being a professional employee can mean being on time to work and treating coworkers with respect and dignity. However, when you know that someone with high-functioning autism, for example, has challenges with these behaviors, where do you draw the line? This can create difficulty in terms of inclusion because typically-functioning (for lack of a better term) staff find it challenging to work with coworkers who are not always respectful. Yet, one thing that has remained important at Spectrum Designs Foundation is respect and dignity for all staff, no matter their differences. Everyone who works at the organization understands that they put people first and look beyond any kind of ability.

Lessons Learned

- Core values are the foundation of a truly diverse and inclusive culture. They also serve as the lens for everything from interviewing and performance management to rewards.

- Inclusion inherently requires some type of accommodation and balance between what the company wants and what an employee needs.

- Taking a non-traditional approach to evaluating applicants can mean the difference between choosing a capable person who has no connection to the mission or culture, and finding a diamond in the rough who has a powerful connection to your company's values.

RESOURCES, TEMPLATES, AND TOOLS FOR WORKFORCE PLANNING
(Items in italics can be found in the appendix.)

Succession Planning

Hassan Abdelkahar Selim, "Identifying Key Positions Within Your Organization: Succession Planning!" https://www.linkedin.com/pulse/identifying-key-positions-within-your-organization-hassan

Employee Development Career Plan Template

Succession Planning Policy

Workforce Planning

Academcy to Innovate (AIHR), "11 Key HR Metrics." https://www.analyticsinhr.com/blog/11-key-hr-metrics/

EPAY Systems, "HR Statistics, Facts, and Trends," https://www.epaysystems.com/hr-statistics/

Carolyn Hirschman, "Putting Forecasting in Focus: A Case Study on Workforce Planning," https://www.shrm.org/hr-today/news/hr-magazine/pages/0307cover.aspx

National Institutes of Health, Office of Human Resources, "Guide: How to Identify Key and Mission-Essential Positions," https://hr.nih.gov/sites/default/files/public/documents/working-nih/workforce-planning/docx/04-keyandmissionessentialpositionsguide-508.docx

Society for Human Resource Management, "Workforce Analytics and HR Metrics," https://www.shrm.org/hr-today/trends-and-forecasting/special-reports-and-expert-views/pages/workforce-analytics.aspx

US Bureau of Labor Statistics, "Labor Force Statistics from the Current Population Survey: Labor Characteristics," https://www.bls.gov/cps/lfcharacteristics.htm

The World Bank, "DataBank: [Global] Labor Force, Total," https://data.worldbank.org/indicator/sl.tlf.totl.in

Diversity and Inclusion

Workforce Planning: Position Justification Form (Budgetary)

SHRM Knowledge Domain(s): Organization; Strategy
Functional Areas: Workforce Management; Business & HR Strategy

ADDITIONAL TOOLS

Exhibit 5.1. Key Person Profile

Name of the person:	Current job level/Code:
In current job since:	Location:
Languages (list):	Nationality:

Previous work outside and inside the organization		
Job/Location	Title	Dates

Key achievements (list):

Competency profile in present job:		
Competency/Behavior	Assessment Method	Proficiency Level

Competency profile for the next level:		
Competency/Behavior	Assessment Method	Proficiency Level

Performance management:
This year's scores (if available):
Last year's scores (if available):
Previous year's scores (if available):
Career goals (if known):
Risk of loss to the organization:
Development needs (list):
Approved developmental action required:

SHRM Knowledge Domain(s): Organization; Strategy
Functional Areas: Workforce Management; Business & HR Strategy

Exhibit 5.2. Key Position Profile

Title of key position:			
Location:			
Why is this a key position? Explain:			
Job code (if applicable):			
Reports to:			
Reported to by:			
Key duties/ Responsibilities	List details below	How often are these duties demonstrated? (Daily? Weekly? Monthly? Quarterly? Yearly?)	How critical are these duties to job success? 5 = Very important 4 = Important 3 = Somewhat important 2 = Somewhat unimportant 1 = Unimportant
	1		
	2		
	3		
	4		
	5		
	6		
	7		
	8		
	9		
Required education:			
Required experience:			
Other essential qualifications:			

© *Copyright 2020 by William J. Rothwell*

SHRM Knowledge Domain(s): Organization; Strategy
Functional Areas: Workforce Management; Business & HR Strategy

Exhibit 5.3. Strategic Workforce Planning Worksheet

Use this worksheet to help organize strategic workforce planning in your organization. Write your answer(s) in the right column for each question in the left column below. Add paper as necessary. There are no right or wrong answers in any absolute sense; rather, some answers may be better than others depending on how well they shed light on the needs of your organization and spur you to action.

Questions	Your Answers
1 How many people does the organization employ at present?	
2 What kind of people does the organization employ at present?	
3 How many people are needed in the future to achieve the organization's strategic goals?	
4 What kind of people are needed in the future to achieve the organization's strategic goals?	
5 What are the present gaps between labor supply and labor demand?	
6 What are the future gaps between labor supply and labor demand?	
7 How can gaps between present labor supply and present labor demand be closed?	
8 How can gaps between present and future labor supply and present and future labor demand be closed?	
9 How can the success of closing present and future gaps be evaluated?	
10 What talents are demonstrated by people in the organization?	
11 How many people have what kind of talents?	
12 What competitive advantages can be leveraged based on the talents and innovation of the organization's people?	

© *Copyright 2020 by William J. Rothwell*

REFERENCES

Dias, Murillo de Oliveira and Roberto Aylmer. "Behavioral Event Interview: Sound Method for In-depth Interviews." *Arabian Journal of Business and Management Review* 8, no. 1 (2019): 1–6.

Direction BV. "What is Inclusiveness?" Accessed May 31, 2019. https://www.management-development.com/article/ what-is-inclusiveness/?cn-reloaded=1.

Edwards, Martin, and Kirsten Edwards. *Predictive HR Analytics: Mastering the HR Metric.* 2nd ed. London: Kogan Page, 2019.

Gliddon, David G., and William J. Rothwell. *Innovation Leadership.* New York: Routledge, 2018.

Rothwell, William. "Replacement Planning: A Starting Point for Succession Planning and Talent Management." *International Journal of Training and Development* 15, no. 1 (2011): 87–99.

Rothwell, William, Peter Chee, and Jenny Ooi. *The Leader's Daily Role in Talent Management: Maximizing Results, Engagement and Retention.* Singapore: McGraw-Hill Education Asia Collection, 2015.

Rothwell, William, James Graber, and Neil McCormick. *Lean but Agile: Rethink Workforce Planning and Gain a True Competitive Advantage.* New York: AMACOM, 2012.

Rothwell, William J., James Graber, David D. Dubois, Aileen G. Zabellero, Catherine Haynes, Ali Habeeb Alkhalaf, and Sarah J. Sager. *The Competency Toolkit.* 2nd ed. Amherst: HRD Press, 2015.

Rothwell, William, and Jim M. Graber. *Competency-Based Training Basics: A Complete How-To Guide.* Alexandria: ASTD Press, 2010.

Rothwell, William and H.C. Kazanas. *Planning and Managing Human Resources: Strategic Planning for Human Resource Management.* 2nd ed. Amherst: HRD Press, 2003.

Rothwell, William, J. and John E. Lindholm, J. "Competency Identification, Modeling and Assessment in the USA." *International Journal of Training and Development* 3, no. 2 (1999): 90–105.

The Conference Board. "Council Perspectives: Insights from The Conference Board Council on Workforce Diversity." Accessed June 2, 2019. https://www.conference-board.org/pdf_free/councils/TCBCP005.pdf.

van Vulpen, Erik. "11 Key HR Metrics." Accessed June 2, 2019. https://www.analyticsinhr.com/blog/11-key-hr-metrics/.

Waters, Shonna D., Valerie N. Streets, Lindsay A. McFarlane, and Rachael Johnson-Murray. *The Practical Guide to HR Analytics: Using Data to Inform, Transform, and Empower HR Decisions.* Alexandria: Society for Human Resource Management, 2018.

West, Mike. *People Analytics for Dummies.* Hoboken: For Dummies, 2019.

ENDNOTES

1. William Rothwell and H.C. Kazanas, *Planning and Managing Human Resources: Strategic Planning for Human Resource Management,* 2nd ed. (Amherst: HRD Press, 2003). See also "What is Inclusiveness?," Direction BV, accessed May 31, 2019, https://www.management-development.com/article/what-is-inclusiveness/?cn-reloaded=1.
2. William Rothwell and H.C. Kazanas, Planning and *Managing Human Resources: Strategic Planning for Human Resource Management,* 2nd ed. (Amherst: HRD Press, 2003).
3. William J. Rothwell and Jim M. Graber, *Competency-Based Training Basics: A Complete How-To Guide* (Alexandria: ASTD Press, 2010).
4. William J. Rothwell and John E. Lindholm, "Competency Identification, Modeling and Assessment in the USA," *International Journal of Training and Development* 3, no. 2 (1999): 90–105.
5. William J. Rothwell, James Graber, David D. Dubois, Aileen G. Zabellero, Catherine Haynes, Ali Habeeb Alkhalaf, and Sarah J. Sager, *The Competency Toolkit,* 2nd ed. (Amherst: HRD Press, 2015); William J. Rothwell and John E. Lindholm, "Competency Identification, Modeling and Assessment in the USA," *International Journal of Training and Development* 3, no. 2 (1999): 90–105.
6. Murillo de Oliveira Dias and Roberto Aylmer, "Behavioral Event Interview: Sound Method for In-depth Interviews," *Arabian Journal of Business and Management Review* 8, no. 1 (2019): 1–6.

7. William Rothwell, "Replacement Planning: A Starting Point for Succession Planning and Talent Management," *International Journal of Training and Development* 15, no. 1 (2011): 87–99.
8. William Rothwell, James Graber, and Neil McCormick, *Lean but Agile: Rethink Workforce Planning and Gain a True Competitive Advantage* (New York: AMACOM, 2012).
9. William Rothwell, Peter Chee, and Jenny Ooi, *The Leader's Daily Role in Talent Management: Maximizing Results, Engagement and Retention (Singapore: McGraw-Hill Education Asia Collection,* 2015).
10. Martin Edwards and Kirsten Edwards, *Predictive HR Analytics: Mastering the HR Metric,* 2nd ed. (London: Kogan Page, 2019); Shonna D. Waters, Valerie N. Streets, Lindsay A. McFarlane, and Rachael Johnson-Murray, *The Practical Guide to HR Analytics: Using Data to Inform, Transform, and Empower HR Decisions* (Alexandria: Society for Human Resource Management, 2018); Mike West, *People Analytics for Dummies* (Hoboken: For Dummies, 2019).
11. "What is Inclusiveness?," Direction BV, accessed May 31, 2019, https://www.management-development.com/article/what-is-inclusiveness/?cn-reloaded=1.
12. "Council Perspectives: Insights from The Conference Board Council on Workforce Diversity," The Conference Board, accessed June 2, 2019, https://www.conference-board.org/pdf_free/councils/TCBCP005.pdf.
13. David G. Gliddon and William J. Rothwell, *Innovation Leadership* (New York: Routledge, 2018).
14. David G. Gliddon and William J. Rothwell, *Innovation Leadership* (New York: Routledge, 2018).

Appendix

All items in this appendix are reprinted with permission and are the copyright of the Society for Human Resource Management. These resources and more are available online at www.shrm.org although member login may be required.

HIRING CHECKLIST

Candidate Name:
Job Title:
Department:
Hiring Manager:

Pre-Offer Checklist
☐ Resume received
☐ Application form completed
☐ References checked
☐ Drug test passed
☐ Background check passed

Post-Offer Checklist
☐ Written job offer accepted
☐ Pre-placement physical passed
☐ Start date confirmed
☐ Office/work space assigned
☐ Office/desk furniture ordered
☐ Basic office supplies ordered
☐ Phone/Extension assigned
☐ Computer/Laptop assigned
☐ Necessary software installed
☐ Monitor/Keyboard/Mouse assigned
☐ Printer/Fax/Copier access created
☐ Network access/passwords created
☐ Email account created

☐ Name badge created
☐ Keys for office/building assigned
☐ Cell phone assigned
☐ New hire announcement written
☐ New hire orientation scheduled
☐ New hire paperwork packet prepared
☐ Safety training scheduled
☐ On-the-job training scheduled
☐ Sexual Harassment training scheduled

Checklist Completed by:
Date:

JOB OFFER CHECKLIST

Offer Specifics
- ☐ Job title
- ☐ Department, manager's name
- ☐ Start date
- ☐ Hours of work/schedule
- ☐ Status (full time, part time, regular, temporary, specific duration)
- ☐ Exempt vs. nonexempt status
- ☐ Rate of pay (hourly, weekly or by pay period) and pay period frequency
- ☐ Contingencies on which the offer may be predicated (e.g., drug testing, reference checking, physical exam, security screen)
- ☐ Paid leave benefits
- ☐ Eligibility for health/welfare benefits plans
- ☐ Work location
- ☐ If travel is involved, approximate percent of travel required
- ☐ At-will employment statement

Attachments (not required but recommended or if based on need)
- ☐ Benefits overview/summaries
- ☐ Job description
- ☐ Blank Form I-9 (bring on start date for completion) with supporting documents
- ☐ An employment agreement, noncompete or other restrictive covenants (bring on start date for completion)
- ☐ Self-identification form (bring on start date for completion)
- ☐ Emergency contact form (bring completed on start date)
- ☐ If travel is involved, summary of company's reimbursement processes

CONDITIONAL JOB OFFER

[Date]
[Candidate Name]
[Street Address]
[City, State, Zip code]

Dear [Candidate Name]:

It is with great pleasure that [Company Name] offers you the position of [job title]. You will be reporting to [Name, Title], and your start date is scheduled for [date].

This is a full-time [exempt position that is not eligible for overtime/nonexempt position eligible for overtime pay after 40 hours in a workweek (include any relevant state daily OT requirements here)]. We are offering you a starting base wage of $_____ [per hour, week] paid [biweekly, semimonthly, etc.].

In addition, your compensation package includes the following (these details are for information purposes and are subject to any policy or plan changes) options:

Eligibility to participate in the company incentive bonus program, subject to the terms and conditions specified in the incentive bonus plan document.

An option for company stock, subject to approval by the Board of Directors and the terms of the company's stock option plan.

Eligibility for health and dental coverage, 401(k) plan and flexible spending accounts, subject to plan terms.

Eligibility for company-paid benefits such as life insurance, short-and long-term disability and long-term care, subject to applicable waiting periods.

Paid time off (PTO) earned on an accrual basis.

Company-paid holidays.

This job offer is contingent upon the following:

[insert any or all of the following:]

Completion of a satisfactory background check.

Passing a drug test.

Satisfactory reference checks.

Execution of an employment/noncompete/confidentiality agreement.

Obtaining _____ level security clearance.

Obtaining _____ certification/licensure.

[If applicable, add:
Once the above contingencies are successfully completed, this job offer will also be contingent upon receipt of results of a satisfactory physical examination designed solely to determine your physical ability to perform the duties of the position being offered to you.]

On your first day, you will be given an orientation by Human Resources. This orientation will include completing employment forms, reviewing fringe benefits, introduction to management and touring the premises. Please bring appropriate documentation for the completion of your new-hire forms, including proof that you are presently eligible to work in the United States for I-9 Form purposes. Failure to provide appropriate documentation within three days of hire will result in immediate termination of employment in accordance with the terms of the Immigration Reform and Control Act.

Please indicate your acceptance of our offer by signing below and returning one copy of the letter, with your original signature, to me no later than [date]. If you have any questions about this offer, please contact [Name, Title] at [phone and e-mail].

We look forward to having you as part of our team and believe you will find this opportunity both challenging and rewarding.

Sincerely,

[Insert name]
[Insert title]

I have read and understood the provisions of this offer of employment, and I accept the above conditional job offer. I understand that my employment with [Company Name] is considered at will, meaning that either the company or I may terminate this employment relationship at any time with or without cause or notice.

This offer shall remain open until [date]. Any acceptance postmarked after this date will be considered invalid.

Date: _____
Signature: _____

UNCONDITIONAL JOB OFFER

[Date]
[Candidate Name]
[Street Address]
[City, State, Zip code]

Dear [Candidate Name]:

We are pleased to offer you the position of _____ at [Company Name] reporting to [Name, title].

This position offers a biweekly salary of $_____, which is the equivalent of $____ on an annual basis. This position is considered exempt under the federal and state wage and hour laws, which means you are not eligible for overtime pay beyond your salary.

[OR]

This position offers an hourly rate of $__.__, which is paid on a weekly basis. This position will be considered a nonexempt position, which means that you will be eligible for overtime time pay for hours worked in excess of 40 in a given workweek [add in any relevant state OT laws here].

This is a full-time position, and hours of work and days are [insert schedule]. Occasional evening and weekend work may be required as job duties demand.

Full-time employees are eligible for company benefits, including __ [days/weeks] of vacation, which is accrued at the rate of _____ hours per biweekly pay period. We also offer health, dental and vision benefits, sick leave, company holidays and a 401(k) plan. A summary of company benefits is enclosed with this letter. Further details will be provided at the new-hire orientation program, scheduled during your first week on the job.

Your employment with our company is at will, which means that either you or the company may terminate the relationship at any time.

As previously discussed, [day, date] will be your first day of employment with us. Kindly indicate your understanding and acceptance of our offer by signing below and returning a copy in the enclosed envelope no later than [date]. This employment offer expires as of [date]. Should you have any questions, feel free to contact [name] at [number].

We look forward to seeing you on [date].

Sincerely,

_____

I accept the offer of employment set forth above.

Signature: _____   Date: _____

TEMPORARY JOB OFFER

[Date]
[Candidate Name]
[Street Address]
[City, State, Zip code]

Dear [Candidate Name]:

On behalf of [Company Name], I am pleased to offer you a temporary short-term position as [position title], expected to last from [beginning date] to [ending date].

As we discussed, in this position your compensation will be $[XX] per hour. This position will be considered a nonexempt position for purposes of federal wage and hour law, which means that you will be eligible for overtime time pay for hours worked in excess of 40 in a given workweek.

This position is regularly scheduled to work approximately __hours a week on the ___ shift. Your work hours are from _____ to ___ Monday through Friday.

Under the terms of [Company Name]'s benefits plan and policies, you will not be eligible for company benefits due to the shorter duration of your employment with the organization.

This offer of temporary short-term employment, if not previously accepted by you, will expire seven days from the date of this letter. If additional time for consideration is necessary, please make this request as soon as possible. If you wish to accept the offer, please sign below and return the letter to me within the prescribed time.

We recognize that you retain the option, as does [Company Name], of ending your employment with [Company Name] at any time, with or without notice and with or without cause. As such, your employment with [Company Name] is at will, and neither this letter nor any other oral or written representations may be considered a contract.

Should you have any questions, please do not hesitate to contact me or [Name], director of Human Resources.

Sincerely,

[Signature of Company Official or HR Director]

I accept the offer of temporary employment set forth above.

_____   _____
Signature   Date

TELEPHONE PRE-INTERVIEW SCREENING FORM

Date:
Candidate:
Interviewer:
Position applied for:
Minimum qualifications:
Desired competencies:

This is [name] from [Company Name]. I am calling in response to the application you submitted for [position title]. Are you still interested in being considered for this position?

I'd like to ask you some preliminary questions at this time to help us in our interview selection process. This will take approximately 10-15 minutes. Is this a good time for you to talk? [If not, ask the candidate to provide a time within the next 24 hours when he or she would be available for a phone screening.]

Why are you interested in working for our company?

What reasons do you have for leaving your current (or most recent) job?

Have you ever been involuntarily terminated? If yes, explain.

Based on what you know about the position we are recruiting for, what skills and experience do you have directly related to this position?

What would your previous supervisors say are your strengths? What about weaknesses?

What work accomplishment are you most proud of?

What are your salary requirements?

This position is [FT/PT] with an expectation to work [number of hours per week and days of work]. Are you able to work that schedule?

If offered a position, when would you be available to start? What questions can I answer for you?

Comments (describe how the candidate's responses relate to the desired competencies for the job):

Interviewer evaluation score (1-4):
★candidates with scores of 3 or 4 will be given additional consideration in the selection process.

1–Does not meet minimum qualifications
2–Meets minimum qualifications but does not possess minimum desired competencies
3–Meets minimum qualifications and possesses some desired competences
4–Meets minimum qualifications and possesses many desired competencies

EMPLOYMENT REFERENCE REQUEST FORM (PHONE)

[Verify that the applicant has provided permission before conducting reference checks and complete this top section initially from candidate's application, resume or interview notes.]

Candidate Name_____
Reference Name_____
Company Name_____
Dates of Employment: From:_____ To:_____
Position(s) Held_____
Salary History_____
Reason for Leaving_____

[Explain the reason for your call and verify the above information with the supervisor, including the reason for leaving. Note any differing or new information below.]

Please describe the type of work for which the candidate was responsible.

How would you describe the applicant's relationships with co-workers, subordinates (if applicable) and superiors?

Is the candidate more of an individual contributor, or is he or she more team-oriented? Why do you think so?

Was the candidate in a lot of high-pressure or stressful work situations? If so how did the candidate handle these situations?

How would you describe the quantity and quality of output generated by the candidate?

What were the candidate's strengths on the job?

What were the candidate's weaknesses on the job?

What is your overall assessment of the candidate?

Did the candidate have any warnings or discipline regarding unexcused attendance issues (frequent absences, tardiness, etc.)? [Do not ask about or discuss medical issues.]

The candidate has applied for a position as a _____ with our company. o you believe the candidate would be a good fit for this type of position? Why or why not?

Would this individual be eligible for rehire at your organization? Why or why not?

Is there anything I haven't asked about that someone considering this person for a job should be aware of?

Completed by: _____ Date: _____

EMPLOYMENT REFERENCE REQUEST FORM (MAIL)

[Name of Reference]
[Title of Reference]
[Reference Company Name]
[Address]

Regarding: [Candidates Name]

Dear:

We are contacting you to verify employment of the above individual with your organization. This individual has applied with our organization for the position of [Position Title]. Attached please find a copy of the applicants signed consent form releasing prior employers to provide our organization information on [his/her] employment history, salary and performance. We appreciate your time and attention to this matter. If you have any questions, please contact me directly at [phone number and email address].

Sincerely,

[Name, Title]
[Company Name]

[Candidates Name]

Dates of employment (month/year): Start Date: _____ End Date: _____

Job title(s): _____

Primary job duties: _____

Quality of work: _____

Was it a voluntary or involuntary separation of employment? _____

Reason for employment separation: _____

Eligible for rehire? (circle one) Yes / No. If No, why? _____

Above information was completed by:

Company Name: _____
Printed Name: _____ Title: _____
Signature: _____ Date: _____

TOTAL COMPENSATION STATEMENT

As an employee of {Company/Organization name}, you receive regular pay for the services you provide. The other part of your total compensation is the value of the benefits that {Company/Organization name} makes available to you and your family. The value of these benefits is your "hidden paycheck." This personalized benefits statement describes your hidden paycheck and is intended to give you a summary of the benefits you personally receive and their value.

If you find any inaccuracies or have questions concerning your benefits and this statement, please contact Human Resources.

Please realize that this personalized benefits statement is not a legal document. All benefits are governed by the actual benefit plans, which have precedence over the information reported in this statement. {Company/Organization name} reserves the right to change, suspend, or cancel its benefit policies or practices with or without notice.

Employee Name: _____

Date of Birth: _____

Social Security No: _____

Date of Employment: _____

Current Salary/Rate: _____

Marital Status: _____

No of Dependents: _____

Medical Benefits

You have elected {insert type/level} coverage for {medical, dental, vision}. {Company/Organization name} pays {amount} percentage of the cost of coverage for a total of {amount} per month.

Flexible Spending Accounts

You have elected to contribute {amount} per pay period to your Health Care Reimbursement Account, which allows you to pay for your eligible health care expenses on a pre-tax basis.

You have elected to contribute {amount} per pay period to your Dependent Care Account, which allows you to pay for your eligible employment-related dependent care expenses on a pre-tax basis.

(continued)

Leave

For the calendar year beginning January 1, your leave benefits include:
Accrued Vacation/Annual Leave: _____
Accrual Rate per Pay Period: _____
Accrued Sick Leave: _____
Accrual Rate per Pay Period: _____
Holiday Leave: _____
Personal Days: _____

The total value of your paid leave for this calendar year (based on your current salary/wages) is {amount}.

In addition, {Company/Organization} has provisions for bereavement leave, jury duty leave, military leave, and family and medical leave.

Disability

If you become disabled because of sickness or accident and are unable to work on a short-term basis, you are eligible to receive {amount} percent of your regular weekly up to a maximum of {amount} per week. {Company/Organization} pays {amount} percent of the short-term disability premium for a total of {amount} per month.

If you are unable to work for long periods of time because of sickness or accident, you are eligible to receive {amount} percent of your regular weekly up to a maximum of {amount} per week. {Company/Organization} pays {amount} percent of the long-term disability premium for a total of {amount} per month.

Life Insurance

You have individual coverage for life insurance in the amount of {amount} times your annual salary. {Company/Organization} pays {amount} percent of the premium cost for a total of {amount} per month.

Employee Assistance Plan

You are eligible to participate in this confidential service, which provides initial professional counseling, and referral services for employees who need emotional, financial, legal, and other types of counseling. {Company/Organization pays {amount} percent of the cost for this benefit for a total {amount} per month.

Social Security

{Company/Organization} contributes to and also forwards employee with-holding taxes under FICA (Federal Insurance Contributions Act which includes Social Security and Medicare benefits) on your behalf. These benefits provide each working American with retirement income and also provide income secu-rity to employees in the event of disability, income security to surviving mem-bers of deceased workers' families, and hospital insurance for the aged and the disabled.

You may request a Personal Earnings and Benefit Statement (PEBES) from the Social Security Administration to verify your earnings records and receive an estimate of your future Social Security benefits.

Retirement

{Company/Organization} sponsors a {type} retirement plan in which you are eligible to participate. You may make pre-tax contributions to the plan and at year-end, based on profitability, {Company/Organization} may make a matching contribution to the amounts you have contributed. You receive a quarterly statement of your retirement benefits through this plan and may also access your personal account information online through {address}.

TOTAL COMPENSATION

As you may have realized after reading the above, your total compensa-tion is significantly higher than your annual salary or wages. The {Company/ Organization's} cost for providing these benefits equals approximately {amount} percent of your salary/wages or {amount} per year.

As your length of employment increases with {Company/Organization}, addi-tional years of service may further enhance the value of benefits, particularly your retirement benefits.

MERIT INCREASE POLICY AND PROCEDURE

Purpose

Each year, the CEO and the chief officers of human resources and finance will determine the pool of merit increase funds available. Both the objectives of the compensation program and financial resources available will be considered in the decision-making process.

Merit pay is used to reward successful performance. Larger merit increases will be awarded to employees who consistently exceed performance standards. Increases will not be granted to employees whose performance has been rated as unsatisfactory overall.

Procedures

Eligibility

To be eligible for a merit increase, an employee must be employed with at least six months of continuous service before the merit award date.

An employee whose pay is at the maximum of the salary range may not be granted an increase that would cause the base salary to exceed the maximum of the range for that position.

Determination of merit increase

In accordance with [Company Name] guidelines, supervisors will recommend: a) whether an employee should receive any merit increase based on his or her annual performance review and b) the amount of increase appropriate for the performance results.

The following factors are the basis for awarding merit pay to employees:
- The employee's performance as reported in the annual performance review.
- The appropriate pay level within the range for the employee considering the employee's performance and performance of others in the range.
- Pay increase funds available.
- Recommendations of supervisors, as approved by executive officers.

Review of merit increase

Merit increases require the recommendation of the employee's immediate supervisor and the approval of the chief human resource officer. Employees are to be notified of their merit increase as soon as possible after all employee merit increases for the year have been approved by the HR director.

Performance reviews

Employee performance is to be formally reviewed at least once each year. The focus of the review is to discuss the employee's performance for the rating period, review standards for the position, communicate the amount of the employee's merit increase and set goals for the next rating period.

PERFORMANCE AND SALARY REVIEW POLICY

Purpose
The performance appraisal process provides a means for discussing, planning and reviewing the performance of each employee.

Performance appraisals influence salaries, promotions and transfers, and it is critical that supervisors are objective in conducting performance reviews and in assigning overall performance ratings.

Eligibility
All full- and part-time employees are provided an annual performance review and consideration for merit pay increases as warranted.
Performance Review Schedule

Performance appraisals are conducted [*annually/quarterly/semiannually*] on [*an established focal date each year / dates announced by HR*]. Each [*Company Name*] manager is responsible for the timely and equitable assessment of the performance and contribution of subordinate employees.

Salary Increases
A performance appraisal does not always result in an automatic salary increase. The employee's overall performance and salary level relative to position responsibilities must be evaluated to determine whether a salary increase is warranted. Out-of-cycle salary increases must be preapproved by the department manager, human resource (HR) director and [*Company Name*] president.

Salary Equity Reviews
A manager may request an analysis of an employee's salary at any time the manager deems appropriate. This request should be made to the HR director, who will review the employee's salary in comparison to other employees in comparable positions and within the guidelines of [*Company Name*]'s compensation policy.

Processes
HR will establish the format and timing of all review processes. The completed evaluations will be retained in the employee's personnel file.

Salary increase requests must be supported by a performance appraisal for salary change processing. Managers may not discuss any proposed action with the employee until all written approvals are obtained.

HR will review all salary increase/adjustment requests to ensure compliance with company policy and that they fall within the provided guidelines.

The HR director has the right to change, modify or approve exceptions to this policy at any time with or without notice.

PERFORMANCE REVIEW MEETING CHECKLIST

☐ Be prepared—know the objectives and goals of the meeting
☐ Time and Place—choose a quiet, private spot with as few interruptions as possible
☐ Conducting the interview
create a positive environment and help the employee feel at ease

give balanced feedback, both positive and negative, but start with the positive

focus on the job, not the person

ask questions and allow the employee to provide feedback

when discussing areas for improvement, discuss methods and objectives for improving

discuss possibilities for advancement, the employee's aspirations and professional development necessary to be a candidate for such future positions

☐ Conclusion
summarize and review the important points of the discussion

restate the action steps that have been recommended and provide a time frame for completion

make sure employee reviews the appraisal and provides comments

have employee sign it to acknowledge that he or she has read it (does not signify agreement with the content)

☐ Follow-up
follow-up with the employee to see how plans are proceeding within the given time frames

offer the employee assistance in achieving objectives and encourage discussion of successes and obstacles

COMPLETED PERFORMANCE APPRAISAL FORM

Employee Name: Terry Jones   **Position:** Marketing Manager
Supervisor Name: Meredith Smith   **Department:** Marketing

Date of employee self-assessment: November 15, 2017
Date of manager assessment: December 5, 2017

Instructions: *Employees are to complete a self-assessment and submit it to their manager no later than November 15. Managers are to complete their assessment and submit it to Human Resources by December 5.*

Rating scale:
 5 Excellent (consistently exceeds standards)
 4 Outstanding (frequently exceeds standards)
 3 Satisfactory (generally meets standards)
 2 Needs improvement (frequently fails to meet standards)
 1 Unacceptable (fails to meet standards)

SECTION 1: OBJECTIVES:
Overall Section Rating: 3.7

Objective	Action Items	Outcomes
Increase number of marketing qualified leads by 15% over prior EOY results.	Lead team to create buyer persona profiles for ideal prospects by Feb. 1. Develop and execute 10-15 "top of funnel" marketing campaigns to generate interest and action from qualified prospects by Dec. 31. Track and report on MQL results on a weekly and quarterly basis to adjust campaigns as needed to achieve the objective.	Four buyer personas were completed on Jan. 30. Fifteen new campaigns were implemented across trade shows, online advertising campaigns and a monthly webinar. MQLs were tracked and reported on weekly. MQLs increased 17.5% over prior EOY results.

Employee Rating: 5	Manager Rating: 5
Employee Comments: The objective was exceeded, and all action items were met and completed on time. Even with one vacant position in the fourth quarter, the team put in extra hours and was able to exceed the goal.	**Manager Comments:** Terry did a great job in designing the action plans and being responsive to needed plan changes. She reassigned and prioritized the workflow when one team member left in the fourth quarter, leading her team to exceed the objective. Plan designs developed this year will be used going forward to build on this success.

Objective	Action Items	Outcomes
Increase conversion rate of marketing qualified leads to sales qualified leads by 5% over prior EOY results.	Develop four nurturing campaigns to engage, educate and inform marketing qualified prospects, at least one per quarter. Modify/enhance campaigns or programs to shorten conversion time by conducting tests on buyer personas. Work with inside sales team to further qualify leads before passing on to field sales team.	Four nurturing e-mail campaigns were launched, targeting our four buyer personas, one per quarter. Conducted two targeted webinars in the first and third quarters. Conducted quarterly tests on buyer personas by varying e-mail frequency and consolidating/spreading out content delivery as warranted. Identified frequencies that consistently increased conversion rates for each persona. Worked with inside sales to refine the processes and timing for when they make first contact with a lead. Overall, conversion rates to sales qualified leads were increased by 4.8%.

Employee Rating: 4	Manager Rating: 3
Employee Comments: While developing and working with new personas, my team was still able to launch successful nurturing campaigns and better determine what frequency of contact showed initial improvements in conversion times. Again, even with one vacant position in the fourth quarter, we came very close to meeting the objective and feel positioned to exceed the rate next year.	**Manager Comments:** Terry led her team in making a great start to increasing the conversion rate of MQLs to SQLs, though they fell just short of the actual objective. This was a solid effort to incorporate new personas and testing frequencies and to build a more efficient process with the inside sales team. These efforts will continue into next year and show signs of being even more effective in years to come.

Objective	Action Items	Outcomes
Increase number of followers on both Twitter and LinkedIn by 15%.	Enhance social media strategies by sharing at least six high-quality content pieces with each persona via social media. Engage with industry influencers and build relationships to increase brand exposure. Partner with industry associations and groups to sponsor social media events.	Each persona received two high-quality content pieces each quarter via Twitter and LinkedIn. A spreadsheet was created to track identified influencers and to show progress in engagement efforts with each. We sponsored two social media events with the leading industry association and organized bimonthly online webchats with interest groups. Overall, followers on Twitter were increased by 22%, while LinkedIn followers increased by 10%.

© Society for Human Resource Management

(continued)

Employee Rating: 3	Manager Rating: 3
Employee Comments: This objective got off to a slower start than the others. We were still able to exceed the goal for Twitter followers but fell short on LinkedIn. With the need to rearrange some priorities, more time was spent on increasing our Twitter presence, so our LinkedIn presence suffered. More time dedicated to social media will be needed in the future to fully realize goals.	**Manager Comments:** As the number of followers increased for both platforms, these results are a success for the objective. Terry made note of the greater effects of more dedicated and consistent time spent on social media platforms and will utilize that knowledge going forward. Terry did a great job of leading her team to increase Twitter followers beyond the goal!

SECTION 2: GENERAL PERFORMANCE REQUIREMENTS:
Overall Section Rating: 4

1. **Job Knowledge** (Applies the technical and professional skills needed for the job.)

Employee Rating: 5	Manager Rating: 5
Employee Comments: Through experience and ongoing education, I bring a high level of marketing and technical skills to the job and keep pace with trends and changes in the industry to continuously improve marketing efforts.	**Manager Comments:** Terry is highly qualified and brings a great deal of experience to her role. She is proactive in staying on top of new marketing technologies, while also staying abreast of industry trends to increase her business acumen, which in turn increases her department's contributions to the bottom line. Terry is a go-to person for the latest innovations and trends.

2. **Communication Skills** (Listens effectively and provides information and guidance to individuals in an appropriate and timely manner.)

Employee Rating: 4	Manager Rating: 4
Employee Comments: I communicate well with my staff, providing weekly status updates on objectives and ongoing feedback to individuals on the team. I have an open-door policy and encourage my team to share opinions openly.	**Manager Comments:** Terry scores well on employee satisfaction and pulse surveys, with above average ratings from her group. When pressed for time, some weekly status updates have been late, but not to any extent to impede the team's progress.

3. **Management Skills** (Guides team to achieve desired results. Delegates responsibilities appropriately and effectively, while developing direct reports.)

Employee Rating: 4	Manager Rating: 3
Employee Comments: I successfully lead my team to achieve objectives by setting appropriate goals, determining workflow and assignments, and keeping the team on schedule. I encourage my team to bring any issues to me, and I resolve them quickly.	**Manager Comments:** Terry is an effective manager who is able to lead her team to achieve or exceed most objectives. While she has a good rapport with her team, she needs to make more time to develop her more inexperienced team members, which will only increase the functionality of the team. Terry will need to focus her efforts at the start of the year on hiring for the vacant position and on coaching current team members to improve their effectiveness.

4. **Organizational Skills** (Sets appropriate objectives to meet commitments within budget. Establishes priorities and organizes workflow to meet objectives.)

Employee Rating: 5	Manager Rating: 5
Employee Comments: I take my financial responsibilities very seriously and always operate within budget. I set and plan my team's action items at the start of the year, taking into consideration the availability of resources and the logical order in which tasks need to be done. Objectives are met or exceeded in most cases and completed on time.	**Manager Comments:** Terry has exceptional organizational skills. Whether it's planning out how to deliver on an objective or organizing the use of her resources, she's up for the task and delivers good-quality work on time. Terry has a remarkable capability in assisting with budget development and in planning work within that budget. All objectives this year were delivered within budget.

(continued)

5. **Initiative** (The degree to which an employee searches out new tasks and expands abilities professionally and personally.)

Employee Rating: 3	Manager Rating: 3
Employee Comments: I think I do a good job of taking initiative at the start of the year, when developing the action plans for my team, and also of staying on top of professional and industry trends.	**Manager Comments:** In terms of setting action plans and keeping the flow of work going, Terry meets all expectations. She also keeps abreast of applicable trends and applies them where possible. In the future, more initiative should be taken to get involved in the overall strategic plan, as opposed to focusing solely on annual objectives. This will help in her development for succession plan purposes.

SECTION 3: PROFESSIONAL DEVELOPMENT:
Section Rating: 3

Pursue the AMA Professional Certified Marketer in Digital Marketing certification by completing three to five LinkedIn Learning courses.

Employee Rating: 3	Manager Rating: 3
Employee Comments: I completed three courses in preparation for taking the Digital Marketing certification exam: Learning Conversion Rate Optimization; Advanced Google Analytics; and Optimizing Marketing E-Mails.	Manager Comments: Three online courses were completed in pursuit of the certification. Terry plans to take the exam next year.

OVERALL RATING: 4

Section 1 (40%):   3.7

Section 2 (40%):   4.0

Section 3 (20%):   3.0

Total Score: 3.68

Employee Signature: Date:

Supervisor Signature: Date:

PERFORMANCE APPRAISAL FORM

Name _____ Job Title_____

Manager _____ Department _____

Review Period From _____ To _____

Purpose of Review:

____Introductory____Annual Performance ___ Other_____

Score the performance in each job factor below on a scale of 5–1, as follows:

5 = Outstanding, consistently exceeds this job factor expectation and is recognized by peers and/or customers as a leader and positive example for others.

4 = Above Expectations, consistently meets and occasionally exceeds this job factor expectation.

3 = Meets Expectations, consistently meets this job factor expectation.

2 = Below Expectations, occasionally fails to meet this job factor expectation.

1 = Needs Improvement, consistently fails to meet this job factor expectation and a job performance improvement plan is required.

Section 1—Job Performance (60% of total score)

Enter up to five job knowledge and skill factors from the job description

SCORE

_____   _____   ____

_____   _____   ____

_____   _____   ____

_____   _____   ____

          _____

Quality of work _____   ____

Quantity of work _____   ____

Negotiable Item _____   ____

Overall Score (Add all scores and divide by the number of factors) × 12 = ____

Comments

_____

_____

_____

(continued)

Section 2—Personal Performance (20% of total score)

Dependability _____ _____

Attendance & Punctuality _____ _____

Interpersonal Skills _____ _____

Flexibility _____ _____

Communication Skills _____ _____

Teamwork _____ _____

Customer Service _____ _____

Negotiable Item _____ _____

Overall Score
(Add all scores and divide by the number of factors) × 4 = _____

Comments

_____

_____

_____

Section 3—Personal Improvement (20% of total score)

Change environment support _____ _____

Quality Improvement support_____ _____

Professional growth_____ _____

Developmental goal accomplishment_____ _____

Negotiable Item_____ _____

Overall Score
(Add all scores and divide by the number of factors) × 4= _____

Comments

_____

_____

_____

Add Overall Scores from Section 1–3 = Total Score _____

Developmental Goals for next review period

1. _____
2. _____
3. _____

Signatures

Employee _____ Date _____

Employee Comments:

_____
_____
_____

Supervisor/Manager _____ Date _____

Department Head _____ Date _____

Human Resources _____ Date _____

PERFORMANCE APPRAISAL FORM
(INCLUDING SUPERVISORY SKILLS)

Employee Name: Position:

Supervisor Name: Department:

Review Period: Date:

Instructions: *Rate the employee's performance during the review period by checking the most appropriate numerical value in each section. To determine the overall performance rating, add the numerical values together and divide by eight (or 11 if the supervisor section was completed). Prior to the performance discussion with the employee, a detailed plan to address areas rated "needs improvement" or "unacceptable" must be submitted to the department head and human resources for review.*

Rating scale:

5   Excellent (consistently exceeds standards)

4   Outstanding (frequently exceeds standards)

3   Satisfactory (generally meets standards)

2   Needs improvement (frequently fails to meet standards)

1   Unacceptable (fails to meet standards)

	5	4	3	2	1
Job knowledge Knowledge of products, policies and procedures; OR knowledge of techniques, skills, equipment, procedures, and materials.					
Quality of work Freedom from errors and mistakes. Accuracy, quality of work in general.					
Quantity of work Productivity of the employee.					

	5	4	3	2	1
Reliability The extent to which the employee can be depended upon to be available for work, to complete work properly, and complete work on time. The degree to which the employee is reliable, trustworthy, and persistent.					
Initiative and creativity The ability to plan work and to proceed with a task without being told every detail and the ability to make constructive suggestions.					
Judgment The extent to which the employee makes decisions that are sound. The ability to base decisions on fact rather than emotion.					
Cooperation Willingness to work harmoniously with others in getting a job done. Readiness to respond positively to instructions and procedures.					
Attendance Consistency in coming to work daily and conforming to scheduled work hours.					

(continued)

Complete this section for employees with supervisory responsibilities:

	5	4	3	2	1
Planning and organizing The ability to analyze work, set goals, develop plans of action, utilize time. Consider amount of supervision required and extent to which you can trust employee to carry out assignments conscientiously.					
Directing and controlling The ability to create a motivating climate, achieve teamwork, train and develop, measure work in progress, take corrective action.					
Decision-making The ability to make decisions and the quality and timeliness of those decisions.					

Noteworthy accomplishments during this review period:

_____

_____

_____

_____

Areas requiring improvement in job performance (attach the performance improvement plan for any areas rated needs improvement or unacceptable):

_____

_____

_____

_____

Actions taken to improve performance from the previous review:

_____

_____

_____

_____

Professional development goals:

_____

_____

_____

_____

Add all numerical values from each category then divide by 8 (or 11 if supervisor section was completed).

Overall performance rating: _____

Employee comments:

_____

_____

_____

_____

Signatures acknowledge that this form was discussed and reviewed.

Employee signature _____ Date _____
Supervisor signature _____ Date _____

PROGRESSIVE DISCIPLINE POLICY

Purpose

[Company Name]'s progressive discipline policy and procedures are designed to provide a structured corrective action process to improve and prevent a recurrence of undesirable employee behavior and performance issues.

Outlined below are the steps of [Company Name]'s progressive discipline policy and procedures. [Company Name] reserves the right to combine or skip steps depending on the facts of each situation and the nature of the offense. Some of the factors that will be considered are whether the offense is repeated despite coaching, counseling or training; the employee's work record; and the impact the conduct and performance issues have on the organization.

Nothing in this policy provides any contractual rights regarding employee discipline or counseling, nor should anything in this policy be read or construed as modifying or altering the employment-at-will relationship between [Company Name] and its employees.

Procedure

Step 1: Counseling and verbal warning

Step 1 creates an opportunity for the immediate supervisor to bring attention to the existing performance, conduct or attendance issue. The supervisor should discuss with the employee the nature of the problem or the violation of company policies and procedures. The supervisor is expected to clearly describe expectations and steps the employee must take to improve his or her performance or resolve the problem.

Within five business days, the supervisor will prepare written documentation of the verbal counseling. The employee will be asked to sign this document to demonstrate his or her understanding of the issues and the corrective action.

Step 2: Written warning

The Step 2 written warning involves more-formal documentation of the performance, conduct or attendance issues and consequences.

During Step 2, the immediate supervisor and a division manager or director will meet with the employee to review any additional incidents or information about the performance, conduct or attendance issues as well as any prior relevant corrective action plans. Management will outline the consequences for the employee of his or her continued failure to meet performance or conduct expectations.

A formal performance improvement plan (PIP) requiring the employee's immediate and sustained corrective action will be issued within five business days of a Step 2 meeting. The written warning may also include a statement indicating that the employee may be subject to additional discipline, up to and including termination, if immediate and sustained corrective action is not taken.

Step 3: Suspension and final written warning

Some performance, conduct or safety incidents are so problematic and harmful that the most effective action may be the temporary removal of the employee from the workplace. When immediate action is necessary to ensure the safety of the employee or others, the immediate supervisor may suspend the employee pending the results of an investigation.

Suspensions that are recommended as part of the normal sequence of the progressive discipline policy and procedures are subject to approval from a next-level manager and HR.

Depending on the seriousness of the infraction, the employee may be suspended without pay in full-day increments consistent with federal, state and local wage and hour employment laws. Nonexempt/hourly employees may not substitute or use an accrued paid vacation or sick day in lieu of the unpaid suspension. In compliance with the Fair Labor Standards Act (FLSA), unpaid suspension of salaried/exempt employees is reserved for serious workplace safety or conduct issues. HR will provide guidance to ensure that the discipline is administered without jeopardizing the FLSA exemption status.

Pay may be restored to the employee if an investigation of the incident or infraction absolves the employee of wrongdoing.

Step 4: Recommendation for termination of employment

The last and most serious step in the progressive discipline process is a recommendation to terminate employment. Generally, [Company Name] will try to exercise the progressive nature of this policy by first providing warnings, issuing a final written warning or suspending the employee from the workplace before proceeding to a recommendation to terminate employment. However, [Company Name] reserves the right to combine and skip steps depending on

(continued)

the circumstances of each situation and the nature of the offense. Furthermore, employees may be terminated without prior notice or disciplinary action.

Management's recommendation to terminate employment must be approved by human resources (HR) and the division director or designate. Final approval may be required from the CEO or designate.

Appeals Process

Employees will have the opportunity to present information to dispute information management has used to issue disciplinary action. The purpose of this process is to provide insight into extenuating circumstances that may have contributed to the employee's performance or conduct issues while allowing for an equitable solution.

If the employee does not present this information during any of the step meetings, he or she will have five business days after each of those meetings to present such information.

Performance and Conduct Issues Not Subject to Progressive Discipline

Behavior that is illegal is not subject to progressive discipline and may result in immediate termination. Such behavior may be reported to local law enforcement authorities.

Similarly, theft, substance abuse, intoxication, fighting and other acts of violence at work are also not subject to progressive discipline and may be grounds for immediate termination.

Documentation

The employee will be provided copies of all progressive discipline documentation, including all PIPs. The employee will be asked to sign copies of this documentation attesting to his or her receipt and understanding of the corrective action outlined in these documents.

Copies of these documents will be placed in the employee's official personnel file.

PERFORMANCE IMPROVEMENT PLAN (PIP) #1

Employee Name:_____

Meeting Date:_____ Dept:_____

Supervisor Name:_____

Standard(s) of Performance Reviewed:
(check all that apply):

☐ [ ] Productivity   ☐ [ ] Attendance
☐ [ ] Efficiency   ☐ [ ] Conduct
☐ [ ] Teamwork   ☐ [ ] Other (define):
☐ [ ] Quality

Specific examples of current performance under review:

Improvement Plan
(what is expected, how it should be accomplished, and in what timeframe):

Acknowledgment:

Employee (signature): _____ Date:_____

Supervisor (signature): _____ Date:_____

(continued)
© Society for Human Resource Management

Periodic Review Notes

Comments	Employee Initials	Supervisor Initials	Date
1.			
2.			
3.			
4.			
5.			
6.			

CHECK ONE:

☐ Performance Action Plan satisfactorily completed on:

_____/_____/_____

☐ Corrective Action Required (attach and submit to Human Resources)

Failure to meet and sustain improved performance may lead to further disciplinary action, up to and including termination. Corrective action may be taken in conjunction with, during, or after the performance plan.

Reviewed and accepted by:

Employee (signature): _____ Date:_____

Review completed by:

Supervisor (signature): _____ Date: _____

Performance Action Plan reviewed by:

Department Manager (signature):_____ Date:_____

Human Resources (signature): _____ Date:_____

This performance plan is not intended to be an employment contract or guarantee of continuing employment.

Copy: Employee
Original: Personnel File

PERFORMANCE IMPROVEMENT PLAN (PIP) #2

To: [*Employee Name*]

From: [*Manager/HR Representative Name*]

Date:

Subject: Notice of Performance Improvement Plan

During the past month [*specify dates if available*], it has become increasingly evident that you have not been performing your assigned work in accordance with what is expected of your position as [*job title*]. You were counseled on this unacceptable performance on [*list dates of all counseling and written warning sessions*]. To date, significant improvement has not been made. [*Company Name*] values you as an employee, and it is our intent to make you fully aware of this situation and to assist you in improving your work performance. The responsibility to improve, however, is yours alone.

You are being placed on a written performance improvement plan. For the next [*30,60, or 90*] days, [*date, 20__*] to [*date, 20__*], your work will be closely monitored. You must demonstrate immediate improvement in the following areas:

[*List plan details. Be specific about what needs to be improved. If possible, list objectives with specific deadlines on a separate sheet and attach it to the plan.*]

[*I or Your manager*] will review your progress on each of the above items requiring improvement every [*day or week and time of review*]. Improvement must begin immediately and be maintained. If any objective of this improvement plan is not met at any time during the specified time frame, disciplinary action, to include separation from [*Company Name*], may occur. A decrease in performance after successfully completing the improvement plan may also result in dismissal from [*Company Name*] without the issuance of another warning or improvement plan.

I am available to discuss any issues or concerns you may have as you work through this plan.

Your signature acknowledges this discussion. It does not indicate agreement or disagreement with this plan.

Employee (signature): _____ Date: _____

Manager/HR (signature): _____ Date: _____

Witness (signature): _____ Date: _____

SEPARATION OF EMPLOYMENT POLICY (VOLUNTARY AND INVOLUNTARY [INCLUDING EMPLOYEE DEATH] TERMINATIONS)

Purpose
It is the policy of [Company Name] to ensure that employee terminations, including voluntary and involuntary terminations and terminations due to the death of an employee, are handled in a professional manner with minimal disruption to the workplace.

At-Will Employment
Employment with [Company Name] is voluntary and subject to termination by the employee or [Company Name] at will, with or without cause, and with or without notice, at any time. Nothing in this policy shall be interpreted to conflict with or to eliminate or modify in any way the employment-at-will status of [Company Name] employees.

Voluntary Terminations
A voluntary termination of employment occurs when an employee submits a written or verbal notice of resignation, including intent to retire, to his or her supervisor or when an employee is absent from work for three consecutive workdays and fails to contact his or her supervisor (job abandonment).

Procedures
1. Employees are requested to provide a minimum of two weeks' notice of their intention to separate employment. The employee should provide a written resignation notification to his or her manager.
2. Upon receipt of an employee's resignation, the manager will notify the human resource (HR) department by sending a copy of the resignation letter and any other pertinent information (e.g., employee's reason for leaving, last day of work).
3. The HR department will coordinate the employee's departure from the company. This process will include the employee's returning all company property, a review of the employee's post-termination benefits status and the employee's completion of an exit interview.
4. Employees who possess a security clearance must meet with the security officer for a debriefing no later than their last day of employment.

Involuntary Terminations
An involuntary termination of employment, including a layoff of over 30 days, is a management-initiated dismissal with or without cause.

Procedures
1. Before any action is taken to involuntarily discharge an employee, the employee's manager must request a review by the termination review board, which consists of the president of [Company Name], a representative from HR and the employee's department head.
2. The termination review board will be responsible for reviewing the circumstances and determining if discharge is warranted. If the board recommends discharge, the employee's manager and an HR representative will notify the employee. The employee's manager should complete an employee change form and notify HR and payroll of the last day worked by the employee.

Death of an Employee
A termination due to the death of an employee will be made effective as of the date of death.

Procedures
1. Upon receiving notification of the death of an employee, the employee's manager should immediately notify HR.
2. The benefits administrator will process all appropriate beneficiary payments from the various benefits plans.
3. The employee's manager should ensure that the payroll office receives the deceased employee's timecard.

Final Pay
An employee who resigns or is discharged will be paid through the last day of work, plus any unused paid time off (PTO), less outstanding loans, advances or other agreements the employee may have with the company, in compliance with state laws. In cases of an employee's death, the final pay due to that employee will be paid to the deceased employee's estate or as otherwise required under state law.

(continued)

Health Insurance

Medical, dental and vision insurance coverage terminates on the last day of the month the employee separates employment or is terminated. An employee will be required to pay his or her share of insurance premiums through the end of the month. Information about COBRA continuation coverage will be provided.

Return of Property

Employees must return all company property at the time of separation, including uniforms, cellphones, keys, laptops and identification cards. Failure to return some items may result in deductions from the employee's final paycheck where state law allows. An employee will be required to sign a wage deduction authorization to deduct the costs of such items from the final paycheck. In some circumstances, [Company Name] may pursue criminal charges for failure to return company property.

Exit Interview

The HR department will contact an employee who voluntarily resigns to schedule an exit interview on the employee's last day of work.

Eligibility for Rehire

Employees who leave [Company Name] in good standing with proper notice may be considered for rehire. Former employees must follow the normal application and hiring processes and must meet all minimum qualifications and requirements of the position, including any required qualifying exam. Rehired employees will not retain previous tenure when calculating longevity, leave accruals or any other benefits, unless required by law.

Employees who are involuntarily terminated by [Company Name] for cause or who resign in lieu of termination are ineligible for rehire. In addition, employees who resign without providing adequate notice or who abandon their job will not be considered for rehire.

FMLA CHECKLIST FOR INDIVIDUAL LEAVE REQUEST

Employee name: _____

Date of leave request: _____

Dates of anticipated leave: _____

☐ Obtain FMLA forms from the U.S. Department of Labor or create similar internal forms.

☐ Determine whether an employee's request for leave is for one of the following FMLA-qualifying reasons:
- The birth of a son or daughter and to care for the newborn child.
- Placement with the employee of a son or daughter for adoption or foster care.
- To care for the employee's spouse, son, daughter or parent with a serious health condition.
- A serious health condition of the employee that makes the employee unable to perform the functions of his or her job.
- A covered family member's active duty or call to active duty in the National Guard or Reserves in support of a contingency operation.
- To care for an injured or ill covered service member.

☐ Within five days of learning of an employee's need for leave that may be FMLA-qualifying, provide the employee with the Notice of Eligibility and Rights & Responsibilities form (WH-381).

Date notice provided: _____

☐ Determine whether the employee is eligible for FMLA leave. An eligible employee is an employee of a covered employer who:
- Has been employed by the employer for at least 12 months.
- Has worked at least 1,250 hours (actual hours worked) during the 12-month period immediately preceding the start of the FMLA leave.
- Is employed at a worksite where 50 or more employees are employed by the employer within 75 miles of that worksite.

☐ Determine whether the employee has used FMLA leave previously and calculate how much FMLA leave the employee has available. An eligible employee is entitled to take up to 12 weeks of FMLA leave during a 12-month period (26 weeks to care for an injured or ill covered service member). The employer's FMLA policy should specifically state which one of the following methods it uses to calculate the 12-month period.

(continued)

The options are:
- The calendar year.
- Any fixed 12-month period, such as a fiscal year or a year starting with the employee's anniversary date.
- The 12-month period as measured forward from the date the employee's FMLA leave first begins.
- A "rolling" 12-month period measured backward from the date an employee uses any FMLA leave.

Has the employee used FMLA leave in the 12-month period as described in the employers FMLA policy? ___ Yes ___ No

If yes, amount of leave remaining: _____

Expected duration of leave: _____

☐ Determine whether a medical certification is necessary and inform the employee if a medical certification is required. If no medical certification is required (e.g., the birth of a child), complete and provide to the employee the Designation Notice (WH-382) within five days of learning of the need for leave.

Date notice provided: _____

☐ If required, provide the employee with the appropriate certification form (one of the following):
- Certification of Health Care Provider for Employee's Serious Health Condition (DOL Form WH-380-E).
- Certification of Health Care Provider for Family Member's Serious Health Condition (DOL Form WH-380-F).
- Certification of Qualifying Exigency for Military Family Leave (DOL Form WH-384).
- Certification for Serious Injury or Illness of Covered Service Member for Military Family Leave (DOL Form WH-385).
- Certification for Serious Injury or Illness of a Veteran for Military Caregiver Leave (DOL Form WH-385-V).

☐ Provide the employee with at least 15 calendar days to return the certification form.

Date certification form due: _____

Date certification form returned: _____

☐ Review the received certification form to ensure that it is complete and sufficient. If information is missing or needs clarification, return the form to the employee with details regarding the information that is needed from the health care provider. Allow the employee at least seven days to return the revised certification form.

Describe any efforts to validate the medical certification: _____
_____

☐ Within five business days after the employee submits a complete and sufficient certification form, provide the employee with the Designation Notice (WH-382).

Date notice provided: _____

DURING LEAVE

☐ Maintain the employee's coverage under any group health plan at the same level and under the same conditions as would be maintained had the employee continued actively working, including employer contributions.

☐ Collect premium payments for health insurance from the employee during periods of unpaid FMLA leave.

☐ Review internal policies to determine how other benefits are impacted by an FMLA absence, such as paid-time-off accruals, life insurance, etc.

☐ Ensure that the employee complies with any requirement for periodic updates to the employer during leave.

RETURN TO WORK

☐ Have the employee obtain a release to work from his or her health care provider, if required.

☐ Reinstate the employee to the same or an equivalent position.

☐ Arrange for the repayment of outstanding insurance premiums owed by the employee.

☐ Maintain records of the employee's FMLA leave for a minimum of three years, separate from the employee's personnel file.

FMLA EMPLOYEE REQUEST FORM

To request leave on the basis of the Family and Medical Leave of Act (FMLA), please complete the following request form and submit to Human Resources at least 30 days prior to leave (unless leave is unforeseen, in which case submit the form as soon as practical).

Employee Name (print clearly): _____

Requested Leave Start Date: _____ Estimated End Date: _____

The reason for this FMLA leave request is (select the most appropriate box):

☐ Birth of a son or daughter and to care for the newborn child.

☐ Placement with the employee of a son or daughter for adoption or foster care.

☐ To care for the employee's spouse, son, daughter or parent with a serious health condition.

☐ A serious health condition that makes the employee unable to perform the functions of the employee's job.

☐ A qualifying exigency arising out of the fact that the employee's spouse, son, daughter or parent is a military member on covered active duty (or has been notified of an impending call or order to covered active duty status).

☐ To care for a covered service member with a serious injury or illness if the employee is the spouse, son, daughter, parent or next of kin of the covered service member.

Time off work is expected to be (select the most appropriate box):

☐ For a continuous block of time (several continuous days, weeks or months off work).

☐ For a reduced work schedule (change in work schedule needed—fewer hours per day or fewer hours per week).

☐ On an intermittent basis (periodic time off that is not usually expected to be the same days or time off from week to week; examples may be time off for flare-ups of a medical condition and/or for ongoing medical treatment/appointments).

Additional information about employee FMLA rights and responsibilities will be provided to you in writing within five business days after receipt of this notice (unless already provided).

Determination of eligibility for leave under the FMLA, and/or additional documentation or clarification of documentation, may be required prior to making a final FMLA determination to approve or deny an FMLA leave request. Please contact Human Resources with any questions.

Employee Signature: _____ Date: _____

Return to Human Resources Department

For HR use ONLY: Date received: _____ FMLA Eligibility Notice sent: _____

FMLA AFFIDAVIT OF FAMILY RELATIONSHIP

In order to approve your request for your leave to be covered under FMLA, [company] is requesting information and documentation of your relationship to the individual for whom you will be caring. Please complete this form and attach relevant documentation as necessary. Return this form to [name] by [date].

Employee Name: _____

Reason for FMLA Leave: _____

Family Member's Name: _____

Relationship to Employee: _____

Family members covered under the federal FMLA include:

- *Parent (biological, adoptive, step or foster father or mother, or any other individual who stood in loco parentis to the employee when the employee was a son or daughter).*
- *Spouse.*
- *Child (biological, adoptive, step or foster children, legal wards, or a child of a person standing in loco parentis of the employee). Note: Child must be either under age 18, or age 18 or older and "incapable of self-care because of a mental or physical disability" at the time that FMLA leave is to commence.*
- *For purposes of military caregiver leave under FMLA, next of kin of a covered service member means the nearest blood relative other than the covered service member's spouse, parent, son or daughter in the following order of priority: Blood relatives who have been granted legal custody of the covered service member by court decree or statutory provisions, brothers and sisters, grandparents, aunts and uncles, and first cousins unless the covered service member has specifically designated in writing another blood relative as his or her nearest blood relative for purposes of military caregiver leave under the FMLA.*

*In-laws, grandparents, siblings and other extended family members are NOT covered by FMLA or company policy unless an in loco parentis relationship exists.

In order to verify that our relationship entitles me to FMLA leave to care for this individual, I have attached a copy of the following:

_____ Birth certificate _____ Marriage certificate

_____ Court document: _____

OR

_____ I certify that the family member for whom I need to provide care for a serious health condition under the FMLA is a covered family member as defined above.

Employee Signature: _____Date: _____

FMLA: EMPLOYER RESPONSE
(when employee has not given advance notice of need for FMLA leave)

Date
Employee Name
Street Address
City, State, Zip Code

Dear [Employee Name]:

On [date], we became aware that you have been absent from work under circumstances that may qualify for leave under the Family and Medical Leave Act (FMLA). The purpose of this letter is to provide you with information and the forms both you and your health care provider need to complete and return to us so that we may determine if your absence(s) may be designated as FMLA leave.

You will find enclosed the FMLA Notice of Eligibility and Rights & Responsibilities and [company name]'s FMLA policy. Please review closely and retain both the notice and our policy.

The following FMLA forms are enclosed:

Employee Request for FMLA Leave: You will need to complete this form and return it to us as soon as possible. A return envelope is enclosed.

Certification of Health Care Provider: You will need to give this form to your health care provider for completion. Your health care provider may return the completed form directly to us (using the enclosed return envelope) or to you for submission. Please be sure that this completed form is returned to us within 15 days following the request or provide us a reasonable explanation for the delay. Failure to provide certification may result in a denial of continuation of leave. As stated in our FMLA policy, medical information received for FMLA leave is considered confidential and shall be disclosed only to those involved in the FMLA leave determination.

After receipt and review of these two forms, we will make a determination on designation of your absence as FMLA leave. If you have any questions or would like more information on FMLA leave, please contact [name, phone number].

Sincerely,

Director of Human Resources

FLSA EXEMPTION QUESTIONNAIRE

[Editor's note: On Sep. 24, 2019, the U.S. Department of Labor (DOL) issued a final rule that set a new salary threshold of $684 a week ($35,568 annualized) for the Fair Labor Standard Act's (FLSA's) white-collar exemption from overtime pay, effective Jan. 1, 2020.]

Note to employers: This questionnaire serves as a basic outline for an employer's initial analysis of positions being considered for exemption under the FLSA, and is meant to serve as one of several tools in such an analysis. Job titles are insufficient to determine exempt status. Additionally, state wage and hour laws may have different requirements. SHRM strongly recommends that employers have legal counsel review their exemption decisions.

Position Title: _____

Employee: _____

Date: _____

Completed by: _____

Completion of this questionnaire helps determine the exemption status of a position. Check the appropriate exemption (executive, administrative, professional, computer-related, outside sales or highly compensated), then check all boxes under the selected exemption that are applicable. To qualify for an exemption, all boxes must be checked for that exemption.

EXECUTIVE (examples: chief executive officer, controller, vice president, director)

☐ Regularly receives a predetermined amount of pay constituting all or part of the employee's salary, which is not subject to reduction because of variations in the quality or quantity of work performed.

☐ Is paid at least $684 weekly (effective Jan. 1, 2020).

☐ Primary duty consists of managing the enterprise or a customarily recognized department or subdivision of the enterprise.

☐ Customarily and regularly directs the work of two or more full-time employees or their equivalents (for example, one full-time employee and two half-time employees).

☐ Has the authority to hire or fire other employees **OR** makes recommendations that carry weight as to the hiring, firing, advancement, promotion or any other change in status of other employees.

ADMINISTRATIVE (examples: manager, supervisor, administrator)

☐ Regularly receives a predetermined amount of pay constituting all or part of the employee's salary, which is not subject to reduction because of variations in the quality or quantity of work performed.

(continued)

- ☐ Is paid at least $684 weekly (effective Jan. 1, 2020).
- ☐ Primary duty consists of performing office or nonmanual work directly related to the management or general business operations of the employer or the employer's customers.
- ☐ Work includes the exercise of discretion and independent judgment with respect to matters of significance.

PROFESSIONAL: LEARNED AND CREATIVE (examples: accountant, nurse, engineer, composer, singer, graphic designer)

- ☐ Regularly receives a predetermined amount of pay constituting all or part of the employee's salary, which is not subject to reduction because of variations in the quality or quantity of work performed.
- ☐ Is paid at least $684 weekly (effective Jan. 1, 2020). (Note: For teachers, licensed or certified practitioners of law and medicine, and medical interns and residents covered under this exemption, the salary basis and salary requirements do **NOT** apply).

Learned Professional

- ☐ Primary duty consists of the performance of work that requires advanced knowledge (beyond high school) and that is predominantly intellectual in character and consistently includes the exercise of discretion and independent judgment.
- ☐ The advanced knowledge is in a field of science or learning.
- ☐ The advanced knowledge was acquired by a prolonged course of specialized intellectual instruction. (This knowledge may be demonstrated either by possessing the appropriate academic degree or by having substantially the same knowledge level and performing substantially the same work as degreed employees but possessing advanced knowledge only through a combination of work experience and intellectual instruction.)

Creative Professional

- ☐ Primary duty consists of the performance of work requiring invention, imagination, originality or talent in a recognized field of artistic or creative endeavor as opposed to routine mental, manual, mechanical or physical work.

COMPUTER-RELATED (examples: network or database analyst, developer, programmer, software engineer)

- ☐ Is paid at least $684 weekly (effective Jan. 1, 2020) **OR** $27.63 per hour. That is, this exemption does **NOT** have to meet the salary basis requirement to regularly receive a predetermined amount of pay constituting all or part of the employee's salary, which is not subject to reduction because of variations in the quality or quantity of work performed **IF** paid at least $27.63 on an hourly basis.

☐ Primary duty consists of:
- The application of system-analyst techniques and procedures, including consulting with users to determine hardware, software or systems functional specifications, OR
- The design, development, documentation, analysis, creation, testing or modification of computer systems or programs, OR
- The design, documentation, testing, creation or modification of computer programs related to machine-operating systems, OR
- A combination of these duties which requires the same level of skills.

OUTSIDE SALES (examples: salespeople, contract negotiators)

The salary basis and salary requirements do **NOT** apply for this exemption. That is, this exemption does **NOT** have the salary basis requirement to regularly receive a predetermined amount of pay constituting all or part of the employee's salary, **AND** this exemption does **NOT** require payment of a minimum salary. Commission-only pay is allowable under this exemption.

☐ Primary duty consists of making sales or obtaining orders for contracts for services or for the use of facilities for which consideration will be paid by the client or customer.

☐ Customarily and regularly is engaged away from the employer's place or places of business.

HIGHLY COMPENSATED EMPLOYEES PERFORMING EXECUTIVE, PROFESSIONAL OR ADMINISTRATIVE DUTIES

☐ Is paid an annual total compensation of $107,432 or more, which includes at least $684 per week paid on a salary basis (effective Jan. 1, 2020). The required total annual compensation of $107,432 or more may consist of commissions, nondiscretionary bonuses and other nondiscretionary compensation earned during a 52-week period, but does not include credit for board or lodging, payments for medical or life insurance, or contributions to retirement plans or other fringe benefits.

☐ Primary duty consists of performing nonmanual office work. Note: No matter how highly paid, manual workers or other blue-collar workers, including non-management construction workers, who perform work involving repetitive operations with their hands, physical skill and energy are not eligible for this exemption.

☐ Customarily and regularly performs at least one of the exempt duties or responsibilities of the executive, professional or administrative exemption.

ADA REASONABLE ACCOMMODATION CHECKLIST

When an employer has information that a disability may be interfering with an employee's ability to perform his or her job, the following steps may be taken:

Identify the need for accommodation.
Unless there is an observable basis or other objective evidence that the employee has an impairment that is affecting job performance, do not inquire about the need for an accommodation.
- Ask the employee if there is any way the employer can assist the employee in the performance of the job tasks. No reference to the Americans with Disabilities Act (ADA) is necessary at this point.
- If the employee declines the need for assistance, no further action is necessary. The employee may be held to the same performance and conduct standards as all other employees.

Engage in the interactive process.
If the employee discloses the need for assistance due to a disability, continue with the following steps.
- Determine whether there is medical documentation or other reliable, objective information to conclude that the employee has a physical or mental impairment that substantially limits a major life activity.
- Review the employee's job description and determine the essential functions of the job. Identify nonessential job tasks that may be reassigned to other employees for purposes of accommodation.
- Discuss possible accommodations with the employee, his or her health care providers, and supervisors who have knowledge of the worksite and the job. Engage other professionals, such as the employee assistance program (EAP) counselors or a vocational or rehabilitation counselor, as appropriate.
- Determine whether the employee's preferred accommodation creates an undue hardship for the employer. If so, suggest and discuss alternative accommodations.

Obtain medical information (if necessary).
When the disability and/or the need for accommodation is not obvious, the employer may ask the individual for reasonable documentation about his or her disability and functional limitations.
- If documentation from a health care provider is necessary, have the employee sign a medical release form.

- Provide the employee with an ADA medical accommodation certification form to be completed by his or her health care provider.
- Provide a copy of the job description to the health care provider and have the provider indicate what major life activity or activities are limited.

Identify the existence of a direct threat.

Direct threat under the ADA is "a significant risk of substantial harm." An assessment of direct threat should be based on valid medical analyses and/or other objective evidence, not on speculation. This is a very narrow exception that may warrant denial of an accommodation and/or termination of employment.

- Determine whether the employee is a direct threat to himself or herself or to others in the performance of the job tasks.
- Document the direct threat by identifying the risk caused by the limitation, the potential harm that could result, and the medical or observable facts on which the risk is based.

Retain documentation.

- Identify and document the reasonable accommodation given, the reason no accommodation was needed or why the accommodation request was denied.
- Keep all medical information in a file that is separate from the employee's personnel file.

REQUEST FOR REASONABLE ACCOMMODATION FORM

NAME: DATE:
WORK PHONE: HOME PHONE:
EMAIL:
POSITION:
DEPARTMENT:
SUPERVISOR/DEPARTMENT HEAD:

NATURE OF THE QUALIFYING DISABILITY:
(Please describe the nature, extent, and duration of your disability.)

REQUESTED/SUGGESTED ACCOMMODATION:
(Please describe the accommodations you believe are needed to enable you to perform the essential functions of this job.)

PHYSICIAN CONTACT INFORMATION (Employees only)
(Please provide name, address, telephone and fax numbers. The physician may receive a letter/fax from us requesting information on your impairment/disability and recommendations for accommodations.)

I authorize the release of necessary confidential medical information regarding my disability to relevant hiring managers as deemed necessary by Human Resources. I also attest to the fact that a copy of the position description has been given to me for review and reference.

Signature:

Date:

[To signatory: In non-physician review cases, decisions regarding accommodations will be made within 10 days of the receipt of this form by Human Resources. Due to delays that may be caused in communications with physicians, no specific decision date can be provided for physician review cases.]

COMMUNICATION TO EMPLOYEE IN RESPONSE TO REQUEST FOR ACCOMMODATION

[Date]

Dear [Employee Name]:

On [Date], you informed [Name and Title] of your medical condition and requested a job accommodation to be able to perform your job functions. [Company Name] complies with the Americans with Disabilities Act (ADA), and we want to support you in continuing to perform your job duties. As part of the process to assist you with your request, we will need the following two items from you:

1. *Your signature on the enclosed medical release form.* This will allow us to discuss your medical condition with your health care provider, if necessary.

2. *A completed certification from your health care provider.* Please take your job description and the medical certification form (enclosed) to your health care provider and review how your medical condition may affect your job functions. Ask your medical provider to indicate in writing what major life activities are limited and to offer suggestions, if any, for the type of accommodation(s) that would assist you with being able to perform your job functions.

Please be assured your medical information will remain confidential. After we have received this information, we will review your accommodation request and respond to you. If you have any questions, please do not hesitate to contact me.

Sincerely,

[Name]

RETALIATION PREVENTION QUESTIONNAIRE

1. Are you prepared for a retaliation complaint?

- Do your non-discrimination and harassment policies cover retaliation and include a strong anti-retaliation statement?
- Do you have a complaint process that employees are aware of, understand, and can follow easily? Do your employees know to whom and how to submit complaints? Do you have a way for complaints to be submitted via an employee hotline?
- Are you training your supervisors on your anti-retaliation policy?
- Do you have an employee relations department or a designated individual to periodically review and implement anti-retaliation policies and procedures, conduct investigations, and provide training?
- Do you consistently and fairly implement disciplinary action?
- Do you keep documentation of all employee performance appraisals and disciplinary actions to document that your practices are fair and not influenced by a complaint of illegal discrimination or other unlawful employment practice?
- Do you keep comprehensive records of all complaints, investigations, and responses?
- Do you discipline and retrain any supervisors who engage in retaliation?
- Do you provide the same information in references for all former employees?

2. Does a potential for retaliation or for a retaliation complaint exist regarding alleged illegal discrimination or other unlawful employer activity exist?

- Is the employee raising informal concerns with a supervisor or manager?
- Is the employee threatening to file a complaint?
- Has the employee filed an internal compliant?
- Has the employee filed a complaint with a state or federal agency?
- Is the employee supporting a co-worker who has filed a complaint?

If the answer is Yes to any of the above,

- Is there any employment action pending on the employee, i.e., promotion, transfer, performance appraisal, demotion, change in job duties, benefits or pay, termination?

- Has the employee asked for a letter of recommendation or reference to be provided to a prospective employer?
- Are any policies or practices being applied differently for this employee?

If the answer is Yes to any of the above, the employers response and action(s), if considered adverse by the employee, may result in retaliation compliant. If a retaliation complaint is received, determine:

- The date of the employment action compared to the date of activity in Section 2 above.
- Documentation of the employees past poor performance or other reason for any adverse employment action.
- If employees in similar situations were treated differently.
- If the person who made the adverse employment action decision was aware of any concern or complaint from the employee alleging illegal discrimination or other unlawful employer activity.

INVESTIGATION SUMMARY REPORT

Date investigation was opened:

Investigator(s) name(s):

Name, title and department of accused:

Description of the allegation (include names, location of incidents, times, dates):

Name, title, department of accuser(s):

Interview timeline (include dates and times of interview, location of interview, names of everyone present). Attach interview notes.

Summary of evidence that confirms or denies allegation:

Applicable employer policy (or policies):

Recommended actions for employer to take:

Actual actions taken by employer:

Date accuser was notified of actions taken:

Date accused was notified of actions that will be taken:

Other post-investigation follow-up conversation(s) (include dates, names and topics of discussion). Attach relevant meeting notes.

Date investigation was closed:

WORKERS' COMPENSATION PHYSICIAN DESIGNATION

OPTION 1
In case of an industrial injury or illness, I elect to receive medical treatment from an Occupational Medicine or Urgent Care Facility provided by my employer.

OPTION 2
In case of an industrial injury or illness, I elect to receive medical treatment from my personal physician.

Personal Physician:

Name _____

Address _____

City_____ State_____ Zip_____

Telephone _____

Employee Name _____

Department _____

Employee Signature _____

Date _____

HR Manager's Signature _____

Date Received _____

UNION-FREE POLICY STATEMENT

[Company Name] is committed to treating its employees with respect and dignity and to providing them with excellent benefits, optimum working conditions and competitive wages. [Company Name] understands that at times employees have concerns and suggestions for improvements. The company encourages its employees to speak up and take advantage of the open-door policy its managers follow. The company listens to its employees and takes their comments seriously.

The direct personal relationship between [Company Name] employees and their managers ensures the best environment for achievement of individual and company goals. [Company Name] believes that a third-party influence would erode its well-established successful employee-manager relationship. A union would not benefit the company's employees, customers or the company.

SUCCESSION PLANNING POLICY

Purpose
Recognizing that changes in management are inevitable, [Name of Company] has established a succession plan to provide continuity in leadership and avoid extended and costly vacancies in key positions. [Company Name]'s succession plan is designed to identify and prepare candidates for high-level management positions that become vacant due to retirement, resignation, death or new business opportunities.

Policy
It is the policy of [Company Name] to assess the leadership needs of the company to ensure the selection of qualified leaders that are diverse and a good fit for the organization's mission and goals and have the necessary skills for the organization.

Procedures
The president/CEO is responsible for [Name of Company]'s succession plan. The president/CEO chairs the Succession Planning Committee, which also includes the executive vice president, the general counsel and the vice presidents of Human Resources and Finance.

1. Each January, a Succession Planning Committee meeting will be held. At each meeting, each division head will:
   a. Present to the Committee a review of the departmental succession plan.
   b. Identify key positions and incumbents targeted for succession planning. This should include an analysis of planned retirements, potential turnover, etc.
   c. Identify individuals who show the potential needed for progression into the targeted positions and leadership within the company.
   d. Outline the actions taken in the previous six months to prepare identified individuals to assume a greater role of responsibility in the future.
2. By the end of February each year, the Committee will approve targeted candidates.
3. By the end of March each year, the Committee will approve an outline of actions that will be taken in the following six months to prepare individuals to assume a greater role of responsibility in the future.
4. The president/CEO will periodically request updates from senior management on the development process for each targeted candidate.

The Committee establishes a succession plan that identifies critical executive and management positions, forecasts future vacancies in those positions and identifies potential managers who would fill vacancies. Vacancies will be filled from within or, in the event no viable candidate is available, on an "acting" basis while an external recruitment effort is conducted.

EMPLOYEE CAREER DEVELOPMENT PLAN
(SUCCESSION PLANNING)

Employee Name:	Current Title:
Current Department:	
Time in Service:	Performance Rating:

Current Duties:

Strengths:	Weaknesses:

Action Plan to Improve:

Training Needs:	Goals:

Promotional position: _____

Ready for promotion (circle one):   Now   in 1-3 years   in 3-5 years

WORKFORCE PLANNING: POSITION JUSTIFICATION FORM (BUDGETARY)

The following information will be used to request additional headcount for your department. This form is to be used for full-time, part-time, temps anticipated for longer than two weeks and intern requests.

Position Title:
Proposed Grade:
Department:
Division:
Supervisor:
Start Month:
____ F/T ____ P/T ____ hours per week
____ Intern ____ Winter/Spring ____Summer ____ Fall/Winter
(Summer term will be budgeted for 37.5 hours/week; spring, fall and winter terms will be budgeted at 20 hours/week)
____Undergrad ____ Master's ____ PhD or Law
____ Temp (List start and end dates) _____
Date Prepared:

POSITION SUMMARY
What are the major responsibilities of this position? Why does this job exist? (Include 2–4 brief, clear, concise statements.)
What major new work will be done with the addition of this new position?
Why won't repurposing existing headcount work?
What is the return on investment that you expect to receive from this position?
How does this position fit in with [company name's] mission and/or what impact does this position have on achieving [company name's] goals and objectives?

KNOWLEDGE/EXPERIENCE
What is the minimum level of education required for this position (i.e., Bachelor's, Associate's, 2-year technical degree)?
Experience in what area(s) would be necessary for this job (i.e., sales, accounting, marketing, customer service)?
In addition to a degree, how many years of experience does this job require?
In lieu of a degree, how many years of experience does this job require?
Skills:
What are the skills necessary for this position?
____ Oral and written communication skills: ____ Good ____ Excellent

_____ Presentation skills: _____ Good _____ Excellent
_____ Decision-making skills: _____ Good _____ Excellent
_____ Problem-solving skills: _____ Good _____ Excellent
Ability to:
_____ Interact in a positive manner with internal contacts.
_____ Interact in a positive manner with external contacts.
_____ Understand verbal/written instructions.
_____ Complete tasks within critical deadlines.
_____ Maintain highest level of confidentiality.
_____ Knowledge/ability to use various software programs (Windows, Outlook, Excel, Word, email, etc.). List software used: _____
_____
_____ Basic math skills.
_____ Other.

FINANCIAL
List the financial responsibilities of the position (i.e., signing authority, expenditures, contract authority, etc.).

SUPERVISION EXERCISED
Which of the following best describes what supervisory responsibility the position has?
_____ No supervisory responsibility.
_____ No direct supervisory responsibility, provides assistance to lower level employees.
_____ Limited supervision, allocates and organizes work, provides guidance.
_____ Direct supervision of at least one employee.
What position(s) does this position have direct responsibility for managing (including recruitment, selection, performance management)?

SALARY FOR THIS POSITION _____
Signatures
Hiring Manager:
Division Chief:
Executive Management Committee :

Please send this completed form to HR
For internal use only (Executive Management Committee)
Date: _____   _____ Approved   _____ Denied
REASON:

Definitions

Absenteeism rate is calculated by dividing the number of missing workers per day over total headcount, multiplied by 100 (absenteeism is predictive of turnover).

Active candidates are people looking for a new role now or soon.

Ad hoc means "on the fly" or "shooting from the hip."

Annual review is a type of performance review that focuses on an employee's yearly job performance.

Behavior, competency, and situation-based questions are open-ended interview questions that require the candidate to answer in detail and describe their approach to a past or potential future event.

Business strategy is an outline of where the company is heading based on a desired outcome, objective, and mission.

Climate, on the other hand, is best understood as "how people feel around here right now."

Core values are established by the company and act as guiding principles on the ways they do business.

Culture boils down to "how we do things around here" and the unspoken expectations that guide behavior. They are the most important things you want your employees to demonstrate when they work

individually, work with others, or represent your company.

Compensation philosophy is the foundation on which a company relies regarding its choices on pay, transparency, and methods of consistently approaching pay equity in the organization. Although it aligns with culture and connects to the business strategy, the compensation philosophy also depends on factors such as the economic conditions and company size, and can therefore change to meet current needs. Sections can include objectives, stakeholder alignment, ethics and culture, risk management, regulatory guidance, and aspects of attracting and retaining talent.

Competencies are individual characteristics that are the foundation for successful or outstanding job performance. They are identified using Behavioral Event Interviews, or critical incidents (stories) collected through an interview process.

Competency-based staff development (or **competency-based training**) is a system where research-based profiles of the present and/or future ideal workers ground development. It centers on making people successful at the work they do by studying people who are successful.

Contingent workers are employed and paid by a staffing agency. These workers complete tasks for a company; however, the staffing firm covers all their performance evaluations, salaries, and benefits.

Contractors provide a service for a company and typically invoice that organization for the tasks performed. They decide what and how something will be done, and the payer only has the right to control or direct the result of the work. Contractors are usually paid a flat fee and are expected to work for a specific timeframe or project. The hiring company's only responsibility to the contractor is to provide payment and to submit a 1099 form.

Critical turnover is calculated by dividing the number of high potential or important worker resignations over the total headcount of high potential or important employees, multiplied by 100.

Delphi process is a way of forecasting needs based on information gathered from several rounds of questionnaires and/or panel discussions.

Dilution is the result of a decrease in the value of equity shares though the process of issuing new equity.

Discipline—otherwise known as *corrective action*—is a common process used to bring employee behaviors into alignment with a company's work rules and requirements.

Employees perform work directly for a company on a full- or part-time basis. The business has the right to instruct the worker and control the work performed, even if the company chooses not to. They are paid a regular wage and are expected to work for an undefined timeframe.

Employee engagement refers to how much passionate commitment people feel about the organizational context, and implies alignment between the individual's and the organization's self-identity.

Equity represents ownership in a company.

Human Resources is defined in two ways:

1. The actual staff or people that work in the company.

2. A strategic function in the company that manages people operations to support successful business outcomes. This involves:

   • Administration of benefits and compensation

   • Supporting recruitment, onboarding, performance management, and training

   • Strategizing retention, workforce planning, diversity and inclusion, risk management, and employee relations

   • Managing change

Hit rate is the percentage of workers listed on succession plans who are actually promoted when vacancies occur.

Inclusiveness is the adherence to six key issues, where leaders are:

1. Open to all ideas

2. Open to all actions

3. Encouraging openness

4. Encouraging open-mindedness regarding all new ideas

5. Remaining tenacious in their actions and demonstrating confidence

6. Encouraging individuals to realize their potential

Incumbents are people currently occupying and performing a roles or jobs in a company.

Introductory reviews examine how well workers perform during the initial months on the job (the introductory period) or after a promotion.

Job analyses document and analyze information about a job to determine the activities and responsibilities it includes, its relative importance to other jobs, the qualifications necessary for performing the job, and the conditions under which the work is performed. The end result of a job analysis is a clearly defined job description.

Job descriptions are used by organizations to communicate talent needs with people outside of the company. It is also a guide to current or future employees as to the scope of the work and performance expectations.

Job grades are groupings of positions with similar worth.

Key people are individuals critical to the organization's operations. The loss of that person would have an outsized, and usually negative, impact on business operations.

Key positions are spots on the organization chart that are critical to the organization's operations.

Mission-driven is a focused approach to doing work that is based on a specific business direction or goal, personal belief, value, or way of being.

Mission statement spells out the reasons the business exists and how it will get work done.

Nondisclosure Agreements (NDAs) are legal documents created to protect sensitive information, including trade secrets and proprietary information.

Ownership percentage is calculated by dividing the number of shares granted by the shares outstanding.

Passive candidates are people not looking for another job right now.

Pay equity is about having a consistently fair approach to compensating different types of employees.

Performance management is a continuing process of communication between workers and their immediate supervisors. The goal is to help plan, monitor, evaluate, and reward behavior and outcomes.

Performance management system involves the policies and procedures made to guide performance management in an organization.

Performance reviews will provide an employee with feedback regarding current work performance and any needs to prepare for future developments.

Positive discipline involves including workers in the decision-making process. It encourages alignment with the organization's behavioral and job performance expectations by showing employees why they must behave and perform in certain ways, and how failure to do so may negatively affect other people or the organization. It documents poor performance by starting with a verbal discussion, then written warnings, and finally an action plan of what you'd like to see happen in a specific timeframe.

Project reviews are performance reviews done at the end of a project by a team leader or by team members evaluating each other.

Risk management is a set of deliberate steps business owners, officers, and managers take to prepare for interruptions to workflow and production.

Small Businesses are for-profit entities that have been in operation for an average of five years and have entered the growth phase. They have a minimum of four full-time employees (including the owners) and generate gross revenues in excess of $250,000 to approximately $1 million in annual revenue.

Social desirability bias occurs when people being questioned answer in a way they think is desirable to the interviewer.

Startups are created to meet an unfilled need in the market. They are typically owned outright by the founders, who also provide the initial funding for operation needs. The founders are the primary staff responsible for doing any and all of the work required in the business.

Strategic workforce planning is a process of identifying the quantity and quality of people needed by an organization over time to achieve its strategic and competitive goals.

Training reviews are performance reviews that can occur periodically (weekly) during a job's training period.

Turnover refers to the percentage of workers who leave during a specific period of time.

Turnover rate is calculated by dividing the number of voluntary resignations over the total headcount, multiplied by 100.

Index